Goal-

LEARNING SUPPORT SERVICES

Please return
on or before
the last date
stamped below

City College
NORWICH

A FINE WILL BE CHARGED ON OVERDUE ITEMS

SAGE HUMAN SERVICES GUIDES

A series of books edited by ARMAND LAUFFER and CHARLES D. GARVIN. Published in cooperation with the University of Michigan School of Social Work and other organizations.

Goal-Focused Interviewing

Frank F. Maple

SHSG SAGE HUMAN SERVICES GUIDES 73

*Published in cooperation with the University
of Michigan School of Social Work*

SAGE Publications
International Educational and Professional Publisher
Thousand Oaks   London   New Delhi

For information:

 SAGE Publications, Inc.
2455 Teller Road
Thousand Oaks, California 91320
E-mail: order@sagepub.com

SAGE Publications Ltd.
6 Bonhill Street
London EC2A 4PU
United Kingdom

SAGE Publications India Pvt. Ltd.
M-32 Market
Greater Kailash I
New Delhi 110 048 India

Printed in the United States of America

Library of Congress Cataloging-in-Publication Data

Maple, Frank F.
     Goal-focused interviewing / by Frank F. Maple.
          p.   cm.—(Sage human services guides; v. 73)
     Includes bibliographical references and index.
     ISBN 0-7619-0180-9 (cloth: alk. paper).—ISBN 0-7619-0181-7
(pbk.: alk. paper)
        1. Social case work.   2. Interviewing.   3. Solution-focused therapy.
     I. Title.   II. Series: Sage human services guides; v. 73.
     HV43.M285   1997
     361.3'22—dc21   97-21126

98 99 00 01 02 03 04 7 6 5 4 3 2 1

Acquiring Editor:	Jim Nageotte
Editorial Assistant:	Kathleen Derby
Production Editor:	Michele Lingre
Production Assistant:	Lynn Miyata
Typesetter/Designer:	Marion Warren
Cover Designer:	Candice Harman
Print Buyer:	Anna Chin

CONTENTS

ACKNOWLEDGMENTS

This book is dedicated to the students at the University of Michigan who have worked with earlier drafts and have provided invaluable feedback in relation to producing the final version.

1

INTRODUCTION

In this book, I want to offer something different from a list of rules or principles for conducting any helping interview. Instead, through the use of scripts from actual cases and descriptions of learning experiences between students and myself, I hope to lead you, the reader, to find your own style of helping others. By placing the major principles of Goal-Focused Interviewing (GFI) within the context of cases or stories, your learning experience may be internalized in a way that allows you to uniquely recapture useful concepts and use them within your own style as you conduct a helping interview.

For example, the major emphasis of GFI is portrayed in the poem below:

> As you go through life, brother,
> Whatever be your goal;
> Keep your eye upon the doughnut,
> And not upon the hole.
> *Anonymous*

As in most poetry, many ideas are included in a short space. Many people focus on what they don't have, on the "holes" in their lives. Others, thankfully, keep their eyes on what they do have, on their strengths and their resources. Helpers can lead them to build on those strengths.

This book focuses on identifying the competencies in helpseekers and in you, the helper. In the stories and cases in which deficits were the focus of any given moment in the treatment setting, you will be given a choice of interventions that will show you how the helper's constructive moves may positively influence the different paths any human interaction may take.

GFI emphasizes a collaborative approach between clients and workers, a win/win type of interaction. In *The Seven Habits of Highly Effective People* (1990), Stephen R. Covey talks about the six paradigms of human interaction. His sixth paradigm, win/win, sees interactions as cooperative, not competitive. This is the paradigm of choice for GFI. When therapists think in constructive or collaborative ways, they tend to lead clients to identify goals that allow clients and therapists to win.

In addition to focusing on possible moves a therapist can use to emphasize a constructive approach, there are some specific procedures included in this book that fit a collaborative approach. These include (a) using a force field diagram to visualize the client's situation, (b) using a silent interview with a client who has chosen not to talk, and (c) consulting with helpers involved in a case.

All the procedures cited above are designed to emphasize that helping is not a contest of power. This may be a new idea to most beginning helpers and to the majority of students. Even many experienced helpers speak about exerting significant control over a client.

As an instructor in interpersonal practice methods classes at the University of Michigan School of Social Work, I have found that many students fit one of two predominant scenarios:

1. Students who think helping involves *getting* people to change, or *making* people see things differently. These students regularly use verbs like *get, make,* and *advise* when talking about their plans for clients in their helping sessions.

2. Students who see clients as begging to be helped, desperately wanting to be saved, cured, or changed. These students use verbs like *show, tell,* and *direct* when talking about what they will do in helping sessions.

Both these scenarios involve a great deal of control on the part of the helper. Yet, being investigated and judged, manipulated, or misled are exactly the experiences family members do not want, as clearly described in the research cited in Reimers and Treacher's (1995) *Introducing User Friendly Family Therapy.*

A student in a class on family therapy who fit the second scenario talked about being surprised that the families he worked with seemed so reluctant to take advice and were so difficult to help. "I thought they would come to therapy eager to improve the problem situation in their family," he said.

To find out how normal this reluctance was, I asked the 28 students in the class to think about their family of origin and to raise their hands if they thought their family could use some family therapy. Almost every hand went up. I then asked the class to raise their hands if they thought it likely that their family of origin would ever seek family therapy. Not one student raised a hand.

This, I believe, reflects the public image of therapy as aversive, stressful, and even humiliating. Because GFI emphasizes a collaborative effort, it is expected to provide pleasure, relaxation, and excitement for both clients and therapists:

When an interview focuses on goals and possibilities for the future, it can seem very pleasurable. When the here-and-now is emphasized as the starting place, this focus allows the helper and the helpseeker to minimize any judgments. These two major themes, starting with where things are now and identifying future possibilities, allow the interviewing experience to be pleasurable and relaxed.

It is unlikely that pleasure, relaxation, and excitement are often achieved in a deficit-focused model. One mother put it very clearly when she was called to schedule a second family session. "I'm not coming back for another mother-bashing session," she said.

The belief that therapy is terribly hard work that can only succeed through extensive pain may have led workers to reach into a client's past and then shove it into the client's face. But certainly a therapy of genuine pleasure, with enjoyable, exciting interactions, is the most desirable form of helping. Any change experience will involve some confrontation, but the total experience of any session should be growth, pleasure and an increased sense of being able to handle problems more effectively by doing things differently.

Such an experience would be different for many "experienced" clients, who have gone through a shopping list of therapists. Yet a different experience is often exactly what these clients are seeking.

It is interesting that many clients today who have worked within a solution-focused model seem willing to "go public" and share their successes in overcoming anorexia, asthma, alcoholism, and so on. These clients find this altruistic effort very empowering in maintaining their own changes. This is quite different from clients secretly seeking help and needing confidentiality because of a humiliating, deficit-focused diagnosis. Obviously, the difference is the joy involved in talking about successful progress in overcoming some negative influence rather than revealing oneself as a victim of one or more deficits.

The key element in any win/win interaction is that the communication is in the receiver's language. For example, I'm a relatively average golfer who has always sought improvement, so I went to a golf professional when I was having more trouble than usual. I told the pro I was bending my elbow too much and swinging too fast. And I was breaking my wrist too soon. I paused, thinking of other mistakes I knew I was making, when the pro interrupted and said, "Show me how you'd like your swing to look."

Well, here I was, demonstrating my very best swing to a golf pro, to appear at my best.

He watched me swing two or three times with my elbow straight, my stroke very slow, and my wrists breaking just about a foot from the ball. And then he smiled and said, "Is that the way you want to swing a golf club?"

"Yes!" I answered emphatically.

"Then you're all set to go out and play. That will be $50."

As you can see, the golf pro elicited my own image about the swing I wanted. He matched my language, inverting my negative words into the way I wanted to swing, without working on my individual errors. He sought my goals and led me to identify what I already knew about swinging correctly.

Compare this approach to the time when social workers proudly thought of themselves as change agents. Taking such a position with every client didn't work because it led to a "pushing" set of strategies that only produced more and more resistance.

For instance, a student presented a case in a case conference involving a very hostile 16-year-old male who just sat for the entire treatment time. The client said "I don't know" to every question she could think of to ask. The group suggested playing something with him. She immediately thought of the games of battleship or checkers as a way to interact with the youth on his rather competitive terms. When she offered him a choice of either game, he chose battleship. His agreement to do anything was a change from his resistant stance.

Many clients, particularly children and adolescents, are pushed into treatment by parents or other authority figures. Working collaboratively with such children usually involves inviting them to do something—anything—with you, rather than attempting to penetrate their resistance.

Any activity is better than trying to "out-silence" an adolescent. For example, the grandson of a friend of mine was seen in therapy for two years, from 12 to 14, and never said one word in a therapy session. Of even greater significance, the youth never told his parents about the "silent therapy," nor did the psychiatrist. After two years, the parents asked for feedback on the therapy's progress. When informed that their son hadn't talked in any session, they withdrew him from therapy. This is an interesting example of a conspiracy of silence, with the therapist's collusion.

The major point of these stories is to suggest that helpers should avoid normalizing any style of communication that doesn't provide progress toward client goals. Normalizing problem ventilation is just as inappropriate as normalizing a "you talk first" approach to therapy. It is up to the worker to find alternative ways of helping, from different forms of verbal interaction, to activities, and possibly to the silent interview as described in Chapter 7. In this way, the worker changes to fit the client.

A final case, described in detail below, may clarify this idea of fitting yourself to the client.

A divorced mother came to a legal aid clinic for help in getting her children back. The children were taken away because the mother was said to be an alcoholic and to be earning her living through prostitution.

The clinic was staffed by law students and social work students in a special project sponsored by the local university. When the mother sat down with the social work student, she clearly stated her goal and her major obstacle:

Mother: I want to get my kids back, and the judge is giving me a hard time.

Social Worker: What does the judge want you to do to get your kids back?

M: Oh you know, the usual stuff. Go to AA and show him I can support them.

SW: Well, let's take one of those at a time. How can you show him you're going to AA?

M: Well, they will give you a note of some kind.

SW: And does he want you to go so many times?

M: Well, he didn't say, but I'm sure I'd have to go twice a week for a while.

SW: How long is a while?

M: Well, I really want the kids back.

SW: And you want to impress him with that wish?

M: Absolutely! I guess I should go three or four times a week for at least a month, and get the notes. That might shorten how long I have to wait to get them back.

SW: OK, sounds like a clear plan. How about showing him you can support them?

M: That's obvious. Get a job—at least a part-time one—to show him I'm trying to do what he wants. It has to be a regular job, one he will accept.

SW: And that's something you can find, a job like that?

M: Sure. There are plenty of restaurant jobs around.

This case emphasizes that joining or matching a client involves collaborating with the client regarding the client's goal and developing a plan to achieve it. With clients who are referred by courts, this involves advocating their interests and finding ways they can get what they want within the system. The worker is not in the role of judging a client's right to "get what they want," so long as what they want is not injurious to themselves or others.

THE BOOK'S FRAMEWORK

The construction of much of this book is in an interactive mode, with the reader given the opportunity to select an intervention at a key moment in a helping session. This framework is intended to help the reader move from a passive mode to active involvement with the material being presented. These actions may internalize many of the ideas provided, leading to the natural adaptations that learners make to "own" the results of their learning.

The cases in the book are presented in script form, with the reader acting as the helper at significant moments in an interview. You, as the reader, will write what you would say at several points of an interview. You are then provided with a menu of four choices from which to select an intervention. You can then read the appropriate page to receive feedback regarding the intervention you selected. You can also look at the rationales for all other menu items. Many of the interventions have been drawn from videotapes of prominent therapists and the writings of many authors. For example, the books on solution-focused therapy—particularly O'Hanlon and Weine-Davis (1989), *In Search of Solutions,* and Scott D. Miller, Mark Hubble, and Barry Duncan (1990), *Handbook of Solution Focused Therapy*—will fit well with this book. In addition, several books by Steve de Shazer, including *Clues* (1988), and Robert Dilts's book, *Changing Belief Systems with NLP* (1990) are particularly helpful in providing more depth than is possible in a book that teaches readers to practice their helping skills. I also recommend reading Lynn Hoffman's (1993) *Exchanging Voices: A Collaborative Approach to Family Therapy,* and *Constructive Therapies: Volume I* (1994), edited by Michael Hoyt.

In particular places in this book, I have referred to Michael White and David Epston. I have found their newsletter and brief articles very valuable in explaining the narrative approach, as well as the writings of many of their associates, particularly Michael Durrant and Kate Kowalski's article (1993), "Overcoming the Effects of Sexual Abuse," which appeared in M. Durrant and C. White (Eds.), *Ideas for Therapy with Sexual Abuse.*

Lastly, I would like to encourage the reader to become familiar with the works of Dr. Edward de Bono, who has written extensively about thinking as a skill that must be learned. I highly recommend his book, *I Am Right, You Are Wrong* (1990) which presents an excellent overview of critical, constructive, and creative thinking.

2

LEARNING GOAL-FOCUSED INTERVIEWING

Learning to be an effective goal-focused helper begins when there is as little uncertainty as possible. Uncertainty can be significantly reduced when you know what you want to do as a helper. The goal-focused approach emphasizes a simple structure, so that the complexities involved are in the interaction between helper and client. The clear, simple structure helps you know what you want to do, and the win/win paradigm can increase your confidence that what you do will be in your client's best interests.

The flow chart for a goal-focused interview includes

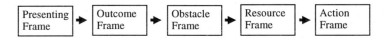

The first step in learning to use the GFI model is to use it on yourself. Your starting point is a desire to improve your level of competency as a helping person. So, ask yourself:

What do I want from being a helper?

or

What are my goals when I work with a client?

Helpers must develop their own goals regarding their body of work. No one can tell you what these goals should be; the goals will evolve from within you as you learn from training programs and actual practice with clients.

But it is possible to suggest a few guidelines to allow helpers to develop their unique goals.

First and foremost, identify goals that focus on both client outcomes and helper satisfaction. For example, a helper might say: "I want to find out what clients want to change in their lives so that I will know we are working on what is important to them."

So please try this idea out. What would you be satisfied with regarding your work in a helping session? Please finish this sentence:

I want to _____
so that _____.

Your sentence may (or may not) look like one of the two examples given below.

1. I want to listen carefully to the client's words, so that I will match the clients language precisely when I respond.
2. I want to ask questions in a proper form that will tend to lead to clearly stated goals.

The goals above contain two of the major principles of GFI. That is, the two goal statements describe matching and leading, the two primary actions that a helper attempts to perform in a goal-focused session.

The first goal emphasizes the helper's effort to speak in the client's language rather than using therapeutic jargon. This is *matching*.

The second goal refers to the helper *leading* a client. In goal-focused interviewing, leading a client means focusing on identifying change goals or finding resources to achieve those goals.

MATCHING

One of the reasons matching is such a powerful experience is that so much of life seems to involve mismatched experiences.

When you ask people about a favorite car, they smile, their eyes sparkle, and they seem to glow with excitement as they describe that car. When you ask adults to name a favorite teacher, they may name three or four out of a possible 50 or 60 teachers.

It is likely that there was something about one car and a few select teachers that clearly matched the person describing these positive experiences. More important, the other cars owned, and the many other teachers, either matched with the person very little or not at all.

In GFI, matching involves connecting precisely with a client's words (auditory, visual, kinesthetic) and the pace of the client's speech. Matching is also important to you as a learner, in that your awareness of your own primary learning style will be vital in all of your training experiences.

We all learn to perform various functions in slightly different ways. You will have to experiment as you read the material in this book to find your natural style. If you're a kinesthetic learner, for example, try closing your eyes as you think about selecting a move with a particular client that you're not connecting with very well. Focus on the desired sensations you wish to experience when you are effectively matching this client, such as feeling confidence, warmth, energy, or pleasure. Now practice delivering a move, and find out if you experience the desired sensation.

If you learn best verbally, write out a move and read it aloud. Then ask yourself if you really understand what this move is intended to achieve. When the outcome can be stated clearly, several other moves will probably occur to you.

If you are a visual learner, picture yourself with the client system and watch them as you deliver the move. You may even want to change a part of one move and try it again to see if it works more effectively.

In addition to learning to make effective moves by using your own natural system, you will want to be very clear about where you wish to lead a client with your key moves.

LEADING

Leading the direction of a worker/client interaction involves taking the client messages and directing them toward the four desired outcomes of GFI.

1. Finding goals and clearly stating them in action terms.
2. Finding strengths and resources that can provide the means to move toward the goals.
3. Eliciting guidelines from clients about their plans to achieve their goals.
4. Eliciting preferences from clients about their priorities in relation to the different aspects of their plans.

To clarify this process, the following example is provided from a videotaped helping session with a student. This tape was made as a live demonstration between a student and myself in a class on interpersonal practice methods.

Frank Maple: What do you want to be happening with your clients that will be different from what is happening now?

Jean: Well, I think, for the most part, I want movement to be taking place for my clients when I'm working with them.

FM: OK, think of one client who you think has shown movement in an interview with you, picture that client, and tell me what you're seeing.

J: (Looks down, pauses for a minute). One of the things that seems to work for me is when I focus on the client's strengths.

FM: And when you do that with this client you're picturing, what do you see happening?

J: She sits up straight, her voice gets louder, and she talks about the things she is capable of doing.

FM: And how is that different from when there is no movement?

J: Well, she usually puts herself down, and talks about how she messed up something she tried to do. Oh, and she hangs her head and talks in a low, whiny voice.

FM: So you want this client, and other clients, to talk about successful experiences and to appear strong and confident in their voice and posture.

J: Exactly! At least more than they are now.

FM: And what will you be doing when clients are talking more confidently?

J: Well, I can't be as unsure as I often am.

FM: So, inside you, you want to be strong and confident?

J: Yeah! It's more like a feeling of an inner balance.

FM: What happens inside you when you have an inner balance?

J: I'm not sure.

FM: Well, let's find some time in your life when you feel sure you had that inner balance.

J: You mean at any time?

FM: Well, it would be nice if you were performing something, like music, or a sport, or . . .

J: Oh, I had it most of the time in field hockey games.

FM: So think about playing field hockey. Picture yourself playing, and nod your head when you have that feeling inside you.

J: (Lowers her head, pauses for a minute, then nods her head). Okay.

FM: So you have it right now—here in this interview with me.

J: Oh yes! It's there right now.

FM: OK, you've got it. Now lose it. Let it go.

J: (Goes inside, head down). It's gone! (Laughing)

FM: How is it different now?

J: Empty!

FM: Please describe the difference between an inner balance and a sense of unsureness.

J: It's almost like a togetherness when the inner balance is there, and when it's not there, it's like a shell, an empty shell.

FM: Are you also picturing that empty shell?

J: Yeah, and that's almost how the therapy goes when I lose it. It's like, you're seeing an empty shell, and you're traveling in the shell, and you're going nowhere.

FM: You did this very well. You found the inner balance, you lost it, so you can get it back when you want it. How do you do that?

J: That's what I'm struggling with. I am in an agency where I have to get background information, and that gets into problem talking. That's what I mean by inner balance. I'm thinking about getting this information and yet I'm trying to focus on client strengths, and that makes it hard to have an inner balance.

FM: So you seem to have come upon a different concern, these agency requirements. Go on with that, please.

J: I'm thinking about what are the dynamics that this person is struggling with, so I can report this to my supervisor. And that makes it hard to be in the here-and-now and let the process flow.

FM: So we've found two goals that seem to be in conflict. And you are trying to do both of them at the same time in an interview with a client. How could you work on each goal at a different time?

J: Gee, I don't know. (Pause) I guess I could think about what happened in the interview after it was over and write down the problem stuff that came out.

FM: Would that work?

J: It might. Oh, and I could tape record the interview so I wouldn't have to worry about remembering things.

FM: What would happen if you did that?

J: (In a loud voice) I could really focus on the client when the interview was going on.

FM: That sounds very strong—you sound like we could stop here and get some feedback from the class. Do you have some sense of closure now, Jean?

J: Oh yes! I found some resources . . . and I found them myself . . . my inner balance and focusing on the here-and-now. And dealing with my supervisor's needs after the interview.

This transcript clearly identifies a few principles for becoming a competent helper. First and foremost, it demonstrates the importance of identifying obstacles that may be hindering you in using your resources. Second, it shows how you can find additional resources by looking back to your life experiences. These past experiences may seem very unrelated to your perception of helping, but if they include the two key ingredients listed below, they have immense potential for moving you toward becoming more competent.

1. The experience involves a situation in which you performed some act, preferably one that you performed often. It can be skiing, surfboarding, tennis, acting in a play, or myriad other human performance activities.
2. The example is drawn from something you successfully accomplished, something you were relatively good at, in your own and others' eyes.

To relate this concept to yourself as a helper, stop a minute and think about your life experiences. Ask yourself, What have I done in some activity where I felt satisfied with my performance? Write your answer below.

_____

_____

Carefully look at what you wrote. Think about how you learned to accomplish this performance competently. What external resources helped you learn to accomplish this performance competently? Write down two or three resources below.

_____

_____

Now ask yourself, what internal strengths helped me to accomplish this performance competently? Write these strengths below.

_____

_____

As you look over what you have written above, get in touch with how you compare with Jean. Are you experiencing a sense of confidence about yourself as you read about your past successful behaviors?

Yes ___   No ___

If yes, take that internal feeling and place yourself in a helping situation with a friend, a relative, or a client. Picture that situation clearly, with you in the picture. Then ask yourself, Do I see myself handling this situation somewhat better than I thought I could?

Yes ____   No ____

If you answered yes, you may now see how drawing from past successes can dramatically and positively influence your confidence in a helping situation.

If you answered no to either question 1 or 2, go back to page 13 and find a past experience different from the one you first identified. That first past experience simply didn't transfer for you to a helping situation. See if a second experience can work for you, to some degree, by working through the steps cited above.

Of course, you can also identify potential resources without going back to things you did competently in the past that were unrelated to a helping situation. For instance, many people drawn to a helping profession have excellent listening skills. Listening carefully usually helps form significant relationships, which is important in working with people. In the space below, list other resources you can think of that may enhance your work as a helper.

1. _____
2. _____
3. _____
4. _____

I can't guess exactly what you may have written, but students, when asked this question, have said things such as showing concern, empathy, and being nonjudgmental.

There are many more resources that could be cited but let's move to the next step.

You have now identified two key elements of a goal-focused approach: (a) clear, well-stated goals, and (b) the resources that will help you achieve those goals. The next step is to write a plan that describes using the essential resources. You can begin that process by stating two specific actions you plan to take in the near future.

PLAN OF ACTION

I will _____

_____

And I will _____

_____

_____

Look over your plan and be sure you haven't limited your capacity to function as an effective helper. Ask yourself, "What have I listed that I might usually consider unrealistic in relation to how I view myself?" If there are no such "unrealistic" statements, write one now for yourself in the space below.

I will _____

_____

_____

A FEW WORDS ON "REALISTIC GOALS" AND PROBLEM SIZE

Probably the most limiting word in the English language is the word *realistic*. Each of us has thoughts and ideas about what we think is realistic for almost any human performance. Yet every day we read or hear of people who seem to have performed miracles. We tend to think of these people as exceptions who have disproven the belief that most people couldn't run a mile under 4 minutes, or complete a 100-mile run, or carry out other seemingly unrealistic achievements men and women now accomplish every day.

Just as thinking about what is realistic or what is unrealistic tends to limit finding resources, strengths, or choices, the idea that problems can be measured as big or small, simple or deep, leads us to inappropriate helping activities. When we use deep problems as our metaphor, we tend to think of "digging" strategies to get down to these problems. Scott Miller (1990), in a conference (February 1996, Tampa, Florida) on Solution Focused Theory, spoke of thick, dense, or multiple problems rather than deep problems. Even these metaphors may be inappropriate because they put helpers into an attack mode that seems necessary to penetrate a thick or dense problem.

In essence, any word that measures a problem simply reinforces the difficulty in resolving the problem. For example, a "small" problem metaphor denigrates both the client who isn't able to deal with it and a worker using time to work on "superficial" concerns.

SUMMARY

You have now walked yourself through the major steps involved in GFI. When you identified your goals, you completed the outcome frame. You were then led through identifying resources and planning your actions. Because I couldn't ask you to tell me about any obstacles you saw in the way of becoming more competent, I identified two common obstacles students have shared with me—trying to be realistic and labeling the size of problems. Hopefully, you identified enough resources to get around these obstacles.

Now that you have used GFI to help you direct your own work as a helper, you should be ready to read and interact with examples of GFI as used with individuals, groups, and families.

Please remember that this material is designed to provide you with examples of possible moves or interventions you may use with clients. You will want to develop a repertoire of your own moves that fit your unique style of helping. As you become comfortable with drawing from your own repertoire of interventions, you will find yourself reacting to each client message spontaneously, without thinking about what you want to say or what you think you "should" say. A certain amount of awkwardness is natural for beginning helpers, and this state will tend to disappear as you focus on client reactions to your interventions.

The major evidence of your growing competence as a helper will be when you are able to recognize that a client has responded in a way that shows movement toward his or her desired goal. At these moments in an interview, your task is to build on any movement by a client, as often seen in an increase of strength or a higher commitment toward achieving his or her desired changes.

3

GOAL-FOCUSED INTERVIEWING WITH AN INDIVIDUAL CLIENT

This chapter will present a verbatim script from a videotape of the first part of an individual intake interview, which tends to focus on the deficits of the client. Throughout the script, you will be shown possible alternative moves, with some speculation on possible client responses.

You will clearly see how the client's problems become enlarged and more complex, which probably makes it more difficult to help the client change.

The purpose of this chapter is to let the case teach some of the GFI principles. In addition, the material at the end of the chapter illustrates how a worker could write a follow-up letter to strengthen the growth that occurred in the interview.

The interview was done in an outpatient mental health clinic. The female client is 24 years old, single, Caucasian, and a college graduate. She lives alone in her own apartment and works in a travel agency. A friend told her about the mental health clinic and she made her own appointment. She had been in therapy for two years prior to going to Europe. She returned to the travel agency three months ago.

Worker: What brought you into the clinic today?
Client: The problem I want to talk about is, I'm in an unusual relationship that I really think I need to get out of, but I feel like for some reason it's not worked through enough that I can get out of it.

This opening line by the client provides many possible cues that would direct the worker to respond in several ways. For example, here is one simple clarifying move:

Worker: What do you mean, "it's not worked through enough?"

Another possible move, as actually used by the worker, was simply:

Worker: Go on.

Let's see what happened as a result of the actual move, before looking at a few moves that might have quickly focused on finding a client goal.

Worker: Go on.

Client: I'm seeing this man who also happens to be my boss and who's married and who is also seeing two other people, and it just feels really humiliating to me. And I feel real angry about it and I feel really angry at myself that I put up with it and don't break it off. But it's just, I don't know, it's horrible and it's humiliating and it's really confusing. I feel like, I don't know what to trust and I don't know what to believe about what's being said. It's, like, he's got a lot of places to seek comfort, so anyway I try to be effective and to, like, ask him to change, but he can always say "well just leave me, I don't care."

As you can see by the response, the client poured out an extensive amount of information about numerous problems. Carefully read the client's response again and then write statements of two to six words describing each problem cited by the client.

Client Problems:

1. _____
2. _____
3. _____
4. _____
5. _____
6. _____
7. _____

Now compare your list with the one on the next page.

1. I'm humiliated.
2. I'm angry about it (what he's doing).
3. I'm angry at myself.
4. It's horrible.
5. It's confusing.
6. Don't know what to trust (or believe).
7. He can tell her to leave.

These first two client statements show excellent examples of the choices often provided at the beginning of an interview. The worker's choices are (a) to focus on how the client wants his or her life to be different, by finding his or her goal(s); or (b) to find out as many of the client's problems as possible. Clearly, the simple "Go on" directed the client to problem talking. In addition, the worker's head nods encouraged the long response by the client.

Now let's look back at the client's first response. The key words (slightly rearranged) for a goal-focused approach are:

"I really think I need to get out of an unusual relationship I'm in." What might you say to help the client develop this goal more completely?

You: (1) _____

_____

Please compare your move with the choices listed in the menu below.

MENU OF ANSWERS FOR (1):

1. What will your life be like when you're out of the relationship?
2. How have you successfully been able to get out of relationships in the past?
3. Tell me what "getting out" would look like when you were doing it.
4. What will you accomplish by getting out of this relationship?

Any of the four moves listed above would likely elicit more goal information from the client. If successful, this direction may reduce or eliminate all seven problems identified above because every problem she identified was occurring within the relationship.

Let's return to the transcript to see what happened next. The worker responded to the client's second statement by saying:

Worker: So he does have the power over you in this situation.

Client: Yeah!! Well, I've worked there all summer, but I met him about 3 years ago when we were really good friends. And we just hung out all the time. But it seemed like he was pursuing me all the time, he really liked me, and so we would hang out together all the time. And then eventually, I left. I left and went to Europe and then I moved to New York for a year. Then I came back here and I called him and said, "I would really like to work for you again." And he said, "Yeah, well, that's fine," and I knew he was seeing other people when I came back, but I think I kinda just expected to come back and to have him all to myself again.

W: But you didn't have him all to yourself then. You shared him with his wife.

C: Well, I was the first person he had ever gone out with, outside of his marriage, so . . . and you know, he would say, "This is really different, this is really weird that I met you." I got the sense that it was special or that I was special to him and that it wasn't kind of something he did all the time. And now I feel, like it's like, all that talk about being special was like he was lying about it. And I don't want it to be a lie, so now I'm trying to force him to take me back so that everything that happened before wasn't a lie. It seems that the more passive he is, the more he kinda just says, "OK" and kinda pushes me away, the more I want him and the more I want to make him admit that he loves me and that he wants me.

Looking at the client's first long response in this segment of the interview, it seems clear that the purpose of eliciting the past information was to help the worker understand the client's problem. That is, the client explains how she had things the way she wanted them and how much things have changed. The problem is that she doesn't like the way things are now, so one goal is to change things back to the way they were before she went to Europe.

This goal can be considered very difficult or impossible to achieve because it involves her boss changing a situation that he clearly is enjoying as it is. In addition, as many others have surmised, it is almost impossible for a person to change another person.

The second very long client statement also talks about how the client wants to "force him to take me back." This is another impossible goal as it also focused on changing her boss in the way she wishes him to be.

The major purpose of the worker's moves in each of these two moments was to obtain more information about the problem. As each client response shows, more problem information only increased the magnitude of the problem, thus decreasing the hope for change.

The key principle here is that "seeking more information" is not an acceptable reason, in and of itself, for making a move in a helping interview. The litmus test for seeking more information is whether you can cite a reason, or reasons, that the information will help the client get what he or she wants. Worker moves that lead to clarifying a client's goal and direct the dialogue toward finding information that will produce paths toward the goal(s) are moves that fit within the GFI model.

In addition, effective worker moves will tend to be clear, brief statements or questions that help both the client and the worker maintain their focus on an important goal and on the possible paths toward that goal.

Given these principles, let's return to the actual dialogue and look for an opportunity to return the interaction to the client's original goal: "I need to get out of an unusual relationship."

As we join the interaction, the worker is responding to the client's previous line:

Client: I want to make him admit that he loves me and that he wants me.

Worker: I can understand that. If the relationship seemed special the first time, why did you go to Europe?

C: Because I had planned to do that before, for a long time. And I had just graduated from college and I kinda felt that I wanted to do things on my own, I wanted my own things. And back then I wasn't that invested in the relationship. It was him wanting me, and he was great and he was there and we'd hang out together all the time and he really cared about me and that felt really good to me. But I wasn't *that* in love with him that I couldn't leave him.

W: So you could leave when you were in charge of the relationship.

C: I think maybe I was a little bit different then and I was more manipulative and that was—it was like I could manipulate him and I could make him want me. But really there was nothing that was ever going to come out of it and I knew that, and I didn't care because it was just kinda fun to do that.

W: Is this relationship like any other you have had?

C: Well, it seems to me that when people, or with men that I go out with, the more they don't recognize me or refuse to kind of admit who I am, or what I mean to them, that I feel more and more attached to them and want them even more. Like eventually I have to just leave them. You know, like it's a way to save myself.

W: You described yourself as manipulative. What do you mean by that?

C: I guess that it's . . . (Long pause) that I think it's more important for me to control the relationship. Or that's the position that I want to be in, I want to be in the position of being able to lead.

There seems to be an opening here for a goal-focused move. Try one by writing it below:

You: (2)_____

_____

Now compare your move with those below.

1. You are using the pronoun "I" now, so you're back to talking about yourself and what you want. That's great!
2. So let's say you're in a position now regarding this relationship of being able to lead. What will you say or do that will lead you to get what you want?
3. Tell me what you will do to lead this relationship at this time.
4. Well, at the beginning of this interview, you said you were in an unusual relationship that you need to get out of. What would lead you out of that relationship?

In carefully reading each of the four moves above, it is important to clarify the purpose of each move. A purpose is given below for 1 and 2. Please write it in for 3 and 4.

1. This move aims to reinforce the client's movement from talking about her boss to talking about herself. This reinforcement is intended to help her stay focused on herself in the next segments of the interview.
2. This move is intended to use the client's language "being able to lead," and connects that language in an empowering way ("What *will* you say?").
3. _____
   _____
4. _____
   _____

Now please compare your statements with those provided below.

3. This move clearly connects the client's words to the immediate situation at this time, thus matching her and leading her out of the past.
4. This move, my preferred one, restates the client's original goal and inserts her action verb (lead) into that goal, thus placing her in charge of her action.

(All four would be considered "good" moves.)

In giving you these four moves and the four rationales, the emphasis is on the following principles:

1. Match the client's words.
2. Focus on the client's original goal.
3. Emphasize the here-and-now and the immediate future.
4. De-emphasize the past and problem talking.

The principle of de-emphasizing problem talking can be illustrated by looking at a segment of the interview that occurred a few minutes later:

Worker: Tell me about relationships you had in college.

Client: I had a boyfriend in college and our relationship lasted two years. He stayed in it longer than he wanted to. He told me later he was ready to leave after the first year.

Worker: Tell me more about that.

Client: Well, he was really, like, my love. The love of my life, and then he ended up going out with someone else. I got really depressed. I couldn't live up to what he wanted me to be. The whole depression was caused when I saw I couldn't have him. I felt like I couldn't have myself back.

The first worker move above has a very traditional purpose. Please write what you think it is in the space below.

_____

_____

If you said something like, "to find past problematic patterns in order to see the more complete problem picture," you're probably right. From a goal-focused perspective, I see this as finding more problems than the client initially brought to the session. This "problem finding" is clearly illustrated in the segment below.

Worker: Why do you think you got depressed at that time?

Client: Because I, I've always been depressed. I've always gone through periods of severe depression, like even when I was really little, I remember like being 3, 4, and 5 and being very depressed. Just like, you know, feeling, like, really suicidal and feeling that I couldn't wait. I had lots and lots of problems with my mother, especially when I was little. And I see in my male relationships, I see kinda my relationship to her in these relationships in men that I go out with.

Worker: Oh really, how?

Client: That she, well, we have a lot of psychosis in our family. Like my grandmother is completely insane, but really vicious.

Worker: Really, did she ever live with you?

Client: No. But, it was kinda like—that was passed on to us. It was like all her kids tried to escape her, you know, my mom's from England. My grandma lives in England, and Mom had one brother and three sisters and the two of the sisters and her brother and her all live in the United States now. They don't really have any contact with my grandma, and anybody who comes into contact with her ends up really wishing they never met her. And so . . . and just growing up kinda in that, in this craziness, you know, with this crazy woman, I mean, she would, like, you know, there's my mom and her sisters and my mom's, like, second oldest and my grandma would, like, they would be 8 or 9 or 10 years old and she would just take off and leave them for three weeks in London during the war, and maybe she would come back and maybe she wouldn't. Also, she beat them up all the time.

In the literature on solution-focused or constructive therapies, this segment would be called "problem saturation." Both the worker and the client may be overwhelmed at this point of the interview.

AVOIDING PROBLEM SATURATION

To help you maintain a goal-focused stance, let's look at two principles:

1. Avoid directing the client into the past. My experience has shown that the client will lead the interaction into parts of the past that are relevant to achieving the client's goal. When the past has been brought up, the worker's task is to also ask the client to include the successful experiences from the past, rather than simply giving a litany of one failure after another.
2. Ask "why" questions very sparingly, if at all. The answers given to why questions tend to be full of blaming or problem information, including everything from toilet training to possible abuse. In addition, as possible causes for any problem are elicited, the client may experience a sense of being released from taking responsibility for change.

Now look back to what the client wanted help with in her opening statement, and then read the following segment of the interview below.

Worker: How does that create problems between you and your mother now?

Client: I feel like my mother always felt . . . it was very hard for her to stay sane for one thing, because two of her sisters have gone insane and uncles have gone insane. But, I mean, they've all been hospitalized, and her and the youngest sister are the only ones that have never been hospitalized. But she's very, I mean she's a lot better now, just life has been a lot better to her now, in the second half than the first half. But I think especially when we were little she still felt really conflicted over, you know, kind of feeling cheated by life and feeling that, that she was really kind of on her own. I don't think she really felt comfortable relating to people, and so she tried to build like a perfect family for herself. And she was always afraid, I think she always feared that she might be like my grandmother and be insane. She wouldn't let herself acknowledge her own feelings.

This paragraph clearly illustrates the concept of problem saturation. The worker has elicited family of origin material that ends up labeling the grandmother and the mother as insane, thus leaving only one step to move that label to the client, which happens in the segment below. The segment followed several minutes of the client talking about her mother's relationship with her, the coldness of it, and how that led to her having to be careful of depending on someone else.

Worker: So it would be dangerous if Bill (the boss) decided that he really did love you more and he was gonna leave his wife.

Client: Yeah. 'Cause I don't think I would . . . I wouldn't marry him and I wouldn't move in with him.

Worker: No, it's quite a dilemma, I can imagine, for you. You get into competitions in which it is humiliating to lose and that's what your going through right now. It hurts to see these other women in the picture. But on the other hand, it would really be frightening if you won.

Client: Yeah.

Worker: And there aren't too many other places to go, to find any other options. So I think that one of the problems is that you've kind of gotten yourself, without thinking about it, into a no-win situation. No matter what happens you're gonna feel pretty uncomfortable, maybe anxious or depressed, which goes with the humiliation.

Client: Well, I know I still feel horrible, that's the thing, that's why I came in here is because it's like, like, I know that I still feel that way, I still feel like this, it's yuck! Instead of me being able to tell him and get him to accept that I feel that way. Now, instead, I just have stomachaches and headaches and I go into work, but that's still telling me, like, you got to do something about it. So it's like I feel, I get lost in the logic of it because I don't even know how to fight like that.

Worker: So what you really wish from him, I think, is that he really acknowledge how you feel and respond to that.

Client: Yeah, yeah, that's what I want out of him, that's why I feel like I want you to . . .

Worker: Were you ever successful at getting your mother to do that?

Client: No.

Worker: Why do you think you can do this with Bill?

Client: 'Cause I'm crazy. (Laughter)

At this point in the interview, if it had occurred 20 years ago, the worker might have picked up the phone and arranged for in-patient hospitalization of the client, her mother, and her grandmother. Of course, that's an extreme idea, but it emphasizes how eliciting the client's problem-saturated story can lead to terrible labels that imply that no one identified can function as a responsible individual.

Thankfully, almost all interviews have "windows of opportunity" when the focus can quickly move to the client's more immediate goals. This occurs about 10 minutes later, when the client says, regarding her boss:

Client: Well, I want Bill to admit that he's been rotten to me, and frustrated me, and humiliated me.

Worker: And, for him to admit that, he has to behave in a much more adult way.

Client: Yeah, and that's the last thing he's going to want to do.

Worker: Then the real problem is that you're getting nothing but grief in this relationship.

Client: Yeah. I feel like I should stop seeing him, but I still work there. I can stop him from calling me, and I won't do anything with him.

What would you say now, if you were the worker?

You: (3) _____

_____

Now compare your answer with those below to see if it is similar to any of them.

1. Why don't you get a new job?
2. When you stop him from calling you and you don't do anything with him, what will happen then?
3. You seem very strong about not seeing him and stopping him from calling you.
4. You really are stuck on the horns of a dilemma.

Rationales for the Answers for (3) Above:

1. This move is poorly formed in that it asks for the causes preventing the client from seeking a new job. The client hasn't even mentioned considering a different job, and she is fully capable of thinking of such a solution herself.

2. This move reinforces the client's commitment to restrict interaction with her boss and leads her to look into the future that such restrictions will likely produce.

3. This move, the preferred move, simply reinforces the client's resolve about contact with her and allows her to lead the interaction to any next step she wishes.

4. This move places the client in a lose/lose situation without hope. It may lead the client to practically give up on changing anything, or it may elicit a recoil in that the client is determined to find a way out, as done in a structural approach.

APPLYING KEY PRINCIPLES

The rest of the material below will allow you to finish the interview, using some of the principles cited earlier.

You can compare the moves you write in with those provided, and your rationale for your move with the rationales provided. Some of the provided moves will not be "good" moves from a GFI perspective. However, the rationales will explain how these moves either fit other models or are simply common moves found in many transcripts of therapy sessions. It is amazing how many students have locked onto four moves that are commonly used by social workers in films or in television shows.

The four most consistently used moves by students in introductory classes include

1. How did you feel about that?
2. Why?
3. Have you ever thought of (followed by some advice)?
4. "Go on's" (or nonverbal "go on's," such as head nods with eye contact) that lead to more and more problem talking.

I won't comment further here on the outcomes these moves generally elicit from clients. The difficulties inherent in these moves, in relation to a particular moment in an interview, will be spelled out in the appropriate rationales.

Let's return to the client when she was talking about stopping her boss from calling her and not doing anything with him.

Worker: When you stop him from calling and stop doing anything with him, what will happen then?

Client: I'm afraid I'll be doing those things just to manipulate him, to make him want me.

You: (4) _____

_____

Your rationale: _____

_____

MENU OF ANSWERS FOR (4).

1. So you're not ready to give him up.
2. I can understand where you're coming from.
3. So what actions would really come out of your intent to get out of the relationship?
4. Why can't you see stopping his calls and not doing things with him as steps toward getting out of the relationship?

Rationales for the Answers for (4) Above

1. This is a closed statement intended to lead the client to make a decision by answering yes or no. It emphasizes the here-and-now in that the decision will represent her thinking at this moment.
2. This is another move that seems to have been popularized by movies and television. If a worker believes that each individual is unique and experiences life uniquely, it follows that no one can "understand" someone else's situation.
3. This is my preferred move, in that it seeks the ways the client can act that are consistent with her goal.
4. This move does not match the client's beliefs. It looks for causes that prevent the client from changing her beliefs. Seeking these causes is likely to lead the client to justify her beliefs, thus making changing them more difficult.

The interview continues after the worker used the third choice from the menu.

Client: Oh, I don't know . . . maybe finding a different job.

Worker: Maybe!

Client: Well, I've been looking in the newspaper and asking my friends about any opportunities.

Worker: When you get a new job, what will that do to make you feel special?

Client: I could feel special about having myself back.

You: (5)_____

_____

Your rationale:_____

_____

MENU OF ANSWERS FOR (5).

1. What would be the first step in finding a different job?
2. You seem to believe that it is very likely that you can get yourself back.
3. So you'd have yourself back, and that would make you feel special.
4. That's a very different idea from depending on someone else to make you feel special.

Rationales for the Answers for (5) Above:

1. This move is intended to focus on the approach the client has brought up regarding achieving her goal, so that she can begin to plan to carry it out.
2. This move reflects the client's new belief that she can get what she wants rather than staying in a no-win situation.
3. This move connects the key client beliefs that are her overall goals, so that her beliefs can be the basis for taking the actions necessary concerning her immediate goal, to get out of the relationship.
4. This move reinforces the difference between the client's words at this time and the words she was using earlier regarding manipulating Bill so that he would make her feel special.

(All of these are considered good moves from a GFI perspective.)

Below is how the interview might have been concluded, using a goal-focused approach.

Worker: So you'd have yourself back, and that would make you feel special?

Client: Yeah!

Worker: That seems different from having a man want you to make you feel special.

Client: I think so.

Worker: How exactly is it different for you?

Client: What's different is that I would be independent . . . you know, not dependent on others for feeling good.

Worker: That's a big difference. I'd like you to think about that difference for the next couple of weeks, and then call me about whether you want to talk further with me.

Client: I guess that's okay. I feel pretty talked out now.

Worker: (Standing up) Fine. Here's my card. Today's February 12th, so call me around the 26th, if you want to get together.

Client: I'll do that. Thanks for seeing me. Bye.

COMMENTS ON THIS CASE

The major reason most workers have to end an interview in this unfinished manner is that the allotted time is up. When an interaction has used up both the client's energy and the available clock time without a sense of closure, it usually means that the interaction wasn't managed very well. A deficit-focused approach tends to use both energy and time due to talking about more and more problems.

For example, the segment on page 24 provides many examples of focusing on client deficits, thus imbedding the client deeper and deeper in her problem state. The worker even uses the no-win or lose/lose concept by leading the client with a "why" question, which leads to the ultimate reason available for anyone indulging in irrational behavior— "I'm crazy."

A major principle illustrated in the transcript above is that the best communication interaction is when brief messages are exchanged between all parties. The lengthy client responses in this transcript built higher and higher piles of client problem material. This outcome is usually the result of intense worker eye contact and head nodding, which tend to be interpreted by clients as "go on" messages, thus leading to long verbal paragraphs. A sentence-to-sentence communication pattern will be clearly shown in later transcripts.

In contrast to the transcript above, when the worker's goal is to intrude as little as possible in the life of a client while still working with the client on a desired change, many interviews will end with the worker saying:

"I wonder if you think we need to get together again."

or
"You seem to be ready to make the necessary changes to move toward your goal."

In addition to questioning the need for further sessions, the worker can state that a follow-up letter can be expected by the client.

WRITING REFLECTIVE LETTERS

Many workers conducting either single session helping activities or brief therapy will use a reflective letter to take the place of several additional visits. Below, you will find a series of exercises that will help you develop a letter for the client in the case in this chapter.

You will want to look back on segments from the transcript in order to organize some of the major material you wish to cite in your letter.

A reflective letter, in a goal-focused approach, briefly highlights the significant material in each of the four major steps of a goal-focused interview.

The first paragraph would include a statement of the client's goal(s). Client goals will emerge throughout an interview, so there will probably be three or four identified. From the transcript, try your hand at finding other goal statements beside the one listed below:

1. I want to get out of an unusual relationship.
2. _____
3. _____
4. _____

Possible goals you may have written:

1. I want to feel special.
2. I want to make him admit that he loves me and wants me.
3. I want to be in control of the relationship.
4. I want to get myself back.

In the second paragraph of your letter, you may also give feedback about client commitment to a goal, such as:

"I'm impressed with how committed you were at the end of the interview about how you would find a new job so that you could have yourself back."

Now take one of the goals you wrote above and write a one-sentence statement that includes the client's motivation regarding achieving that goal.

_____
_____
_____

For example, you might have written:

"I was amazed at how differently you talked about getting yourself back as a way of feeling special, compared with when you were talking about getting Bill to want you so that you would feel special."

Emphasizing changes or differences that evolved in an interview is intended to reinforce those changes and the client's strength in making them.

A third paragraph in your letter to the client would identify any planning done by her that would move her toward her goal of getting out of the relationship with Bill. In this area you have several items you could mention. Write a couple of sentences below that would identify the client's planning.

_____

_____

_____

You might have written something like the two examples below:

"You've already decided to stop his phone calls, and it will be a real step to getting out of the relationship when you do that."

"I was surprised when you said you were not going to see him outside work."

In addition, you probably mentioned getting a new job. It would also be helpful to add,

"I was wondering whether getting a new job has become the highest priority in your planning."

This last sentence, which is intended to lead the client toward prioritizing her next steps, would be a fine closing statement for your letter. Also, a copy of your letter would be an excellent record of the interview to place in the client's office file.

In summary, a reflective letter contains references to the four major tasks of a worker in GFI:

1. Goals (short-term and overall).
2. Strengths and resources (internal—beliefs, ideas, values; and external—people, significant environments).

3. Plans (steps that will move toward any goal).
4. Priorities (first things first).

In addition, the worker reflects on the client's degree of commitment regarding these four areas, and about how that commitment seemed to become different during the interview.

SUMMARY

This case offers the reader the opportunity to contrast a deficit-focused approach with a goal-focused approach. It is provided to clarify how searching the client's past to find common problematic threads tends to increase the depth of any problem and to reduce hope for the possibilitiy of change. In addition, the case offers the alternative of using a reflective letter in place of one or more face-to-face sessions. In my experience, such letters have significantly contributed to the feeling, by a client, of being valued and respected.

4

GOAL-FOCUSED INTERVIEWING WITH GROUPS

The principles that have been previously described for individual therapy can be easily applied to groups. The best application is one in which *one client at a time* is the focus during any segment of a helping session, with one or two primary helpers. That is, each client may work on his or her concerns for 15 to 20 minutes, with one group member acting as a single helper, or two as co-helpers. Other group members will be observers/participants who reflect after the working session is completed or give input when requested.

As a group worker, you can choose the kind of group you wish to operate from the following paradigm:

	Single Helpseeker	Multiple Helpseeker
Single Helper	Goal-focused Interviewing	Children's Groups
	Gestalt Therapy	Group Psychotherapy
	Behavior Modification	
Multiple Helper	Positive Peer Culture	Support Groups
	Guided Group Interaction	Self-Help Groups

The boxes above give several examples of different theoretical approaches to working with groups. Most of these groups will carry out three activities at their meetings:

Planning

Working

Processing

All group participants in a GFI model will be involved in the planning and processing aspects of a single session. During the working phase, each client in GFI will take a turn presenting something they want to change, usually about themselves or perhaps a relationship they wish to improve. One or two group members will serve as primary helpers. Observing members can be invited to participate at any time.

CASE STUDY 1

To give you a picture of a GFI group session, a transcript is provided below that shows part of the first session of a group of adolescents in a high school setting. The first session is necessarily planned by the worker (in this case coworkers) because the members have no opportunity to plan the first session.

All the members of this group volunteered to work together to *improve key relationships in their lives.* The worker, Ruth Walker, a school social worker, recruited the members from an 11th grade class. She also recruited John Leonard, a male social worker, to join her, as the group was made up of 3 male students and 4 female students.

Ruth's plan for the first session involved 5 steps:

1. Introducing members to each other in a purposeful way, that is, emphasizing a positive resource in their lives.

2. Developing an initial contract with each student regarding one aspect of his or her life he or she would like to improve, such as self, or a relationship.

3. Conducting a goal-focused session for one student.

4. Eliciting reflections from group members.

5. Briefly developing a tentative agenda for the next session.

HOW THE SESSION BEGAN

Ruth and John greeted each group member by name and invited them to sit wherever they wished in the circle of chairs. Ruth gave out name tags so each member could write his or her first name in large letters and place on a shirt or blouse. Everyone had arrived within a few minutes, so the worker began the meeting by introducing herself as Mrs. Walker, and John as Mr. Leonard, and asked each member to give his or her name.

Ruth then asked the members to briefly think about a person in their lives who had most influenced them in becoming the person he or she was "today."

After about two minutes, Ruth asked each member to pair up with someone else. (The seven members moved their chairs to do this, and Ruth asked John to pair up with a member.) She then asked each pair to assign the letter A to one person, and the letter B to the second member of the pair.

Ruth then directed the A group members to talk for about 5 minutes to their partner about one influential person they had thought of during the silent time. The B members were asked to simply listen carefully, so they would remember what they heard.

The A group members quickly began talking to the B members. Ruth found it difficult but managed to stop the interviews after about 7 minutes. She then asked the partners to switch with the B's, telling their partners their stories, with the A members listening carefully.

After the second interviews were completed, Ruth asked the members to introduce their partners to the group by sharing something that impressed them from the interview. Before this introduction was done, however, each member told his or her partner what he or she was going to share, to be sure there was comfort regarding sharing with everyone.

As you look back on this "ice breaking" activity, identify what purposes you believe were accomplished by checking the item in the list below.

1. ___ Tends to identify problems
2. ___ Considerate of privacy (confidentiality)
3. ___ Likely to identify strengths from the past
4. ___ Emphasizes "small talk"
5. ___ Relatively unstructured
6. ___ Moves quickly into talking about important content from each member's life

Answers (2), (3), and (6) were featured in the ice breaker.

THE GO-AROUND

Ruth: Now that we know each other a little bit, I'd like each of you to tell us what relationship you'd like to improve; you know, your reason for joining this group. I'd like to tape record this part of the meeting so we can review your goals down the road. (Ruth checks with each member on whether taping is okay.)

Jean: My relationship with my boyfriend's mother. That's what I want to change.

Carol: I just want to have more friends, make new friends, than I have now.

Bill: I don't really know what's most important right now. I'll pass and think about it during the meeting.

Ruth: Okay, that's fine. I'll check back with you at the end of the meeting today. What?

Ann: I'm not sure either. (Pause) I guess I'd like to change things between me and both my mom and dad. We're fighting a lot.

Ruth: You sound quite clear on that, Ann. Julie, you're next.

Julie: I'm mostly worried about school. I feel like I hate every class I'm in.

Ruth: Does that mean you want to improve your relationship with a teacher or two?

Julie: Yeah, I guess so. I'm not getting along with any of them.

Ruth: Well, we're getting a real variety of different goals that people want help with. What about you, George?

George: I want to talk about how our lousy parents try to run our lives.

Ruth: Okay. Several people nodded their heads when you said that. (Ruth turns and looks at Kim, and simply waits).

Kim: Guess I'm the last one. I'm kinda like George; too much stuff from my mom, and lots of fighting with her.

Ruth: Well, now we've heard from most of you about what you are here to work on, and I'm sure people will find other important areas in which they want change as our group goes on. I'd like to ask someone to volunteer to work on what they want to change to get us started. (Ruth scans the group, then looks up at the ceiling and waits for a volunteer.)

(After a brief pause, Jean leans forward and says, "I'll go first." Ruth asks her permission to tape the work, and receives an "okay" from Jean.)

The Go-Around is designed to set initial general goals for each individual member and give an idea of the purpose each member has for working in the group.

DIRECTIONS FOR COMPLETING THIS CHAPTER

In this chapter, you will act for John, the co-therapist. At 10 places in the ongoing script of the first group session, you will be asked to write in "what you would say now" as if you were actually participating in this first treatment session.

After writing the actual words you would use as your intervention or your move, you will be asked to look at a menu of four choices of possible interventions. Please choose the intervention that comes closest to what you wrote, or choose the one you think would be most helpful at the moment in the session.

After you have selected one of the four choices, you will be asked to turn to the answer page at the end of the chapter regarding all four menu items. The feedback focuses on the intent or purpose of each item. The purpose of each intervention is its intended outcome.

There are an infinite number of possible moves at any given point in a treatment session. I am providing only four at each point where you are asked to intervene. These interventions are simply examples of different types of responses, and are intended to encourage you to broaden your repertoire of interventions for use in your own treatment sessions.

I don't wish to imply that there is a "right" or "wrong" intervention at any particular moment in a session. I do want to encourage you to develop your ideas about some clear purposes for your key interventions. When you have internalized a way of helping people that you can explain to others, including your clients, you will have made progress toward being a more competent professional.

TRANSCRIPT OF GROUP MEETING

Jean: Well, I'm bursting to get this out. I want help on my relationship with my boyfriend's mother. Really, I guess it's my relationship with my boyfriend and how his mother is trying to break us up.

Ruth: Go on.

Jean: Well, my boyfriend, his name is George, and he goes to another school. He's using drugs, and I want him to stop, not because his mom wants him to but because of what the drugs are doing to him. See, his mother thinks I'm a bad influence on him. I'm sure she thinks I'm on drugs but I'm not. I just don't know how to convince her that I'm clean.

Ruth: Seems like there are two relationships you want to change here. Which one should we focus on now?

Jean: Definitely his mother.

Ruth: What will changing your relationship with his mother accomplish?

Jean: Gee, I don't know.

Ruth: What ideas do group members have about what might happen if Jean could change her relationship with George's mother?

Carol: I think both of them want to get George off drugs. There would be a better chance of that if they both worked together on it.

Ruth: Does that make sense, Jean?

Jean: Yes, lots of sense.

Ruth: So, how can you communicate this common side to her?

Jean: I'm scared she'll reject me 'cause this is the first time that I'll be trying to tell her that I'm on her side.

You (1) _____

_____

_____

*Please write in what you would say now, as the co-therapist. After writing a brief intervention (usually one sentence), look at the answers below and select the menu item you think would be most helpful to say *now*. It may or may not be like what you wrote.

Note: Use a half sheet of paper to cover the ongoing transcript, so you can't see what happens in the next few minutes of the meeting.

Answers for (1):

A. ____ Tell us a little about a time when you and George's mother did get along.

B. ____ What do you say at the start of the meeting with the mother?

C. ____ What is it you want the group to do today that will help you in your session with his mother?

D. ____ Why didn't you tell her before that you weren't using drugs?

After checking one item, turn to page 50 to see whether the menu item you chose did have a useful purpose at this moment in the interview.

THE SESSION CONTINUES

Ruth: Tell us a little about a time when you and George's mother did get along.

Jean: When we first started going together, she really liked me. Then George started doing worse and worse in school, and then she found some drugs in his dresser drawer.

Ruth: When she really liked you, what did you talk about?

Jean: She did most of the talking about when she was young. Even about how her husband walked out on her, leaving her with George and his sister.

You (2) _____

_____

_____

Compare your answer with the four provided below, with the ongoing transcript covered. Check one answer that you consider helpful to say now.

Answers for (2):

A. ____ So she's had some big disappointments in her life.

B. ____ What were you doing while she was talking?

C. ____ She must have trusted you then to tell you such personal stuff.

D. ____ How did you feel when she was telling all that stuff?

Now look at page 50 and read the rationales for each of the answers above.

THE SESSION CONTINUES

Ruth: What were you doing while she was talking?

Jean: We were doing dishes together after we had dinner.

Ruth: And when do you do things together now?

Jean: Not much.

Ruth: Anything at all?

Jean: Well, two weeks ago, I was there watching TV at her house before she got home. George was in his room, so I asked if I could help her with anything. We put away the groceries and started dinner, but she was really quiet, so I just left.

You (3) _____

_____

_____

Now compare your answer with the four below.

Answers for (3):

Please check one item.

A. ____ Well, you've changed since then. You've decided to tell her that you want the same thing she wants.

B. ___ So you didn't break the ice then by starting the talking, and starting talking is what you'll have to do in the future.

C. ___ How can you tell her how worried *you* are about George?

D. ___ How would you like her to respond when you tell her you're worried about how to get George to stop using?

Now turn to page 51 for the rationales for each answer.

THE SESSION CONTINUES

Ruth: How would you like her to respond when you tell her you're worried about how to get George to stop using?

Jean: I'd just like her to listen, without getting angry at me.

Ruth: What could you say to her, so she might listen?

Jean: That's where I'm stuck. I have a lot of hurt feelings about her blaming me.

Ruth: This is a good place to ask for help from the other group members. What ideas do some of you have about how Jean could get George's mother to listen?

Carol: It's hard to get parents to listen to us. My mom doesn't listen to me.

You (4)_____

_____

_____

Compare your answer with the four below, and check the one that you think would be most helpful right now.

Answers for (4):

A. ___ Let's try and look for solutions for Jean right now. We can help Carol with her relationship with her mother after we've given Jean some hope in her situation.

B. ___ Okay, Carol has a common relationship problem to Jean. Who's found a way to improve a relationship with an adult?

C. ___ Do you all have communication problems with adults?

D. ___ I remember Jean clearly saying what she wanted: to tell George's mother they were on the same side. Who can think of a way to do that so the mother will listen?

Now look at page 51 and read the rationales for each of the answers above.

THE SESSION CONTINUES

Ruth: Let's try and look for solutions for Jean right now. We can help Carol with her relationship with her mother after we've given Jean some hope in her situation.

Kim: Well, I ask her to sit down near me, and tell her I just wanted her to listen to me, without saying anything.

Ruth: How does that sound to you as you say it?

Jean: I don't even know if I'm strong enough to say that to her.

Ruth: You were strong enough to bring up this situation at our first group.

Jean: Well, I don't know the people like I know her.

You (5)_____

_____

_____

Now compare your answers with the four below, and check the one that you think would be most helpful at this moment.

Answers for (5):

(Notice that group members who were observing were invited to participate by Ruth in the segment above, thus becoming resources for you to use.)

A. ___ Why don't you just give up trying to get along with her?

B. ___ If you don't talk with her, what will happen?

C. ___ Practice what you'd say right now. Tell us where you'd be with her, you know, set the scene.

D. ___ What are you afraid will happen?

Now look at page 51 and read the rationales for each of the answers above.

THE SESSION CONTINUES

Ruth: Practice what you'd say right now. Tell us where you'd be with her, you know, set the scene.

Jean: It would be sometime when we're alone, and I would ask her to sit down for a few minutes, so we can talk. Well, I'd ask her . . .

Ruth: Yes! (Head nod)

Jean: I think I'd really say, I want to say something, and I just want you to listen.

Ruth: Sounds fine.

Jean: Yeah, I just want you to know how worried I am about George and the way he's throwing his life away on drugs.

You (6)_____

_____

_____

Now compare your answer with the four below, and check the item you think would be most helpful at this point in the interview.

Answers for (6):

A. ____ As you hear yourself say that, how do you think it will come across to George's mother?

B. ____ And what do you think she might say back to you?

C. ____ I wonder if group members might comment on Jean's opening sentence.

D. ____ I think your words might make George's mother defensive.

Now look at page 52 and read the rationales for each of the answers above.

THE SESSION CONTINUES

Ruth: And what do you think she might say back to you?

Jean: She might put me down.

Ruth: (Scanning the group) I'd like some of the group members to comment on how they reacted to your opening sentence.

Carol: I think the mother would feel kinda under attack—that you're criticizing her son.

Ruth: Other thoughts. (More scanning)

Bill: I guess I'm thinking like George might, that it's none of their business what I do.

You (7)_____

_____

_____

Now compare your answer with the four below.

Answers for (7):

A. ____ I'm glad to get a point of view from someone like George. Let's hear some other viewpoints.

B. ___ Well, we're here to help Jean find a solution. What do you think, Jean, about what Bill said?

C. ___ Is it your business, Jean?

D. ___ Why don't you think it's Jean's business, Bill?

Pick the answer above that comes closest to what you wrote. Then look at page 57 and read the rationale for the answer you chose, as well as the rationales for the other answers.

THE SESSION CONTINUES

Ruth: Is it your business, Jean?

Jean: What I really want is to stop avoiding things. My relationships are important to me. That's why I joined this group. I want to work on them, not just let them go. I want to learn how you work on a relationship that stinks. Like the one I have with George's mother.

Ruth: Your voice really became louder when you responded to Bill's comment. Seems like it was helpful to you.

Jean: Yes, it was. And the group can help me by telling me what they would say; how they would start out with George's mother. That would really help. I don't want to attack her.

Julie: Tell us something likable about her.

You (8) _____
_____
_____

Pick the answer below that comes closest to what you wrote. Then look at page 52 and read the rationales for each of the answers below.

Answers for (8):

A. ___ How does what he's doing hurt her?

B. ___ You could say to her what you said just now to us.

C. ___ That's probably why she's cool to you.

D. ___ Have you told her that you know it hurts her?

THE SESSION CONTINUES

Ruth: You could say to her what you said just now to us.

Jean: Yeah, I could tell her that.

Ruth: What do other group members think about Jean saying these things to George's mother?

Julie: It sounds better to me than what you said when you practiced. You're kinda connecting to her, and not attacking her.

Ruth: So please try it with us, Jean.

Jean: Okay. Mrs. _____, I just wanted you to know that you really care about George, and that what he's doing is hurting you.

Ruth: I think she'd like to have someone say that. Being a single parent can be a tough job. What else do you want her to hear from you?

Jean: That I'm hurting, too.

Ruth: And . . .

Jean: That I want to find some way to get him to stop the drugs, just like she does.

Julie: What if she accuses you of using, too?

Jean: I'll tell her I don't and I never have.

Carol: How did she get the idea that you use drugs?

Jean: I have no idea.

You (9)_____

_____

_____

Now compare your answer with the four below.

Answers For (9):

A. ___ I'd like to check on Jean's progress in this session, in relation to her goal of improving her relationship with George's mother. What's the single most important thing you want to happen in your relationship with her?

B. ___ We're getting away from the focus on helping Jean improve her relationship with her boyfriend's mother.

C. ___ We'll never be able to figure out how George's mother came to believe that.

D. ___ That's not important. What difference does it make how she came to believe that Jean uses drugs?

Pick the answer above that comes closest to what you wrote. Then look at page 53 and read the rationales for each of the answers above.

THE SESSION CONTINUES

Ruth: I'd like to check on Jean's progress in this session in relation to her goal of improving her relationship with George's mother. What's the single most important thing you want to happen in your relationship with her?

Jean: I want her to respect me, and I'll know she does if she listens to me.

Ruth: And I think you said she used to, when you first started going together.

Jean: Yeah! We got along great early on, but then George wasn't having trouble in school.

Ruth: What about when George's mother told you that you were getting along so well?

Jean: She would answer almost any question I asked her. I felt that I could talk to her easier than my own mom.

Ruth: That sounds really special. Do you think she knew you felt that way?

Jean: No, I'm sure she didn't.

You (10) _____

_____

_____

Now compare your answer with the four below.

Answers for (10):

A. ____ Why didn't you tell her?

B. ____ What do you think her reaction would be if you told her?

C. ____ Then that's something else you could tell her when you ask her to listen to you.

D. ____ Were you afraid to tell her how much you liked her?

Pick the answer above that comes closest to what you wrote. Then look at page 53 and read the rationales for each of the answers above.

THE SESSION CLOSES

Ruth: What do you think her reaction would be if you told her?

Jean: If I told her now, I don't know what she would say.

Ruth: What would you like her to say?

Jean: That she was happy that I felt that way about her.

Ruth: Would that be different from the way she talks to you now?

Jean: Yes!

Ruth: Would that show you the kind of respect you said you wanted from her?

Jean: Sure would!

Ruth: And what are you thinking about doing with her that's different from you've been doing?

Carol: I think in that way you're respecting her, just as you want her to respect you. Do you see it that way?

Jean: I didn't think of it that way before, but it seems clear now.

Ruth: You seem to be clear on what you want to do. What other help do you want from the group?

Jean: Not much, really.

Ruth: Well, then, let's have group members reflect some of the things they experienced this first session. And then we can have a general debriefing of the session.

THE REFLECTING PART OF THE SESSION

Ruth now reminded the group members of the guidelines for reflecting by pointing to a newsprint pad on which she had written.

Do's	Don'ts
• Make specific observations of growth or strength, such as "I saw your eyes light up when" . . .	• Give advice, "You should. . . "
	• Give opinions, "You were really "scared when you said, ' . . . '"
• Reinforce positive resources	• Generalize, "It was a great session"
• Share how the work personally affected you	• Above all, don't judge.
• Above all, be accurate	

After looking over the guidelines, look back at the script and find material that you could state in a message to Jean. Then write a one sentence reflection below.

_____

_____

You can now compare what you wrote with the four messages that were actually shared with Jean:

1. I noticed how different you were later in the session when you were practicing what you were going to say to George's mother. Your voice was strong, and you sat up—even leaned forward.

2. As I listened to you, I really respected how much you care about George, and I think his mother will pick that up from you.

3. Speaking of respect, I'm really respecting you now . . . having the courage to be the first to open up here, and talking about something really serious.

4. To me, you became so much clearer on what you want as you were talking, and more committed to talking to George's mother.

Ruth did not pursue reflections from every member. She asked Jean to simply listen to each reflection without commenting on it. Ruth said that Jean would be asked, in about three weeks, to give the group any feedback she chose to share regarding her situation. At that time, she could also comment on the impact of any of the reflections.

Ruth closed the meeting with an open debriefing process in which each member shared any internal thoughts or feelings he or she had experienced during the meeting. She functioned primarily as a gatekeeper, making sure everyone had an opportunity to speak, and limiting the length of any member's input.

Finally, she reminded the group about the confidentiality of everything shared in group meetings, and told them they would be able to listen to parts of the audiotape at the start of the next session. She emphasized that planning the session would be the first order of business.

VARIATIONS

Now that you have read a very descriptive example of one type of a goal-focused group, it is important to describe variations to the example provided. Every group started by a worker can achieve three major purposes. These purposes (or aims, or goals) can be achieved only through a group experience. For example, (a) when a worker wants to offer clients the opportunity to help other clients, the worker can form a treatment group as a vehicle for clients to assist each other. This helping process also models how to give help and how to receive and use help. (b) Groups also provide a significant increase in the quantity of feedback that each member can receive. And (c) groups have demonstrated the ability to generate far more new ideas than a dyad (client and helper) is capable of generating. (Research has demonstrated that the ratio is about 8 to 1, groups vs. dyads.)

These three qualities allow a group to be an efficient and effective treatment modality. To build on these dimensions, two workers designed their groups as described in the following examples.

CASE STUDY 2

In a public high school, a social worker was asked by the administration to help reduce the dropout rate. Two approaches were identified: (a) to attempt to bring some students back who had already left school; and (b) to prevent students who were thinking about dropping out from actually doing so.

Because the worker wanted to be sure to emphasize strengths in her group sessions, she began with an informal survey among students to find individuals who had dropped out from the high school and had then come back and were presently in school. After finding 11 such students, she interviewed them all to find out (a) if they were glad they came back, and (b) if they would be willing to help her bring other students back to school. Three students agreed to this contract, and also agreed to recruit a few ex-students they knew who seemed likely candidates to return to school for the coming semester.

The social worker then planned five group sessions involving the three volunteers and three people presently not in school. All the sessions focused primarily on ideas for successfully returning to school. The ideas were written down in a Reentry Manual that was then used by other newly formed groups that were all student led. Difficulties that students typically encountered were emphasized in the manual, with suggestions for over-coming each difficulty. The groups were advertised within the school, inviting students who were thinking of dropping out to join a group.

CASE STUDY 3

A second example of a worker creatively using a success-focused model for some group sessions was done in a residential treatment setting for adolescent males. In this particular setting, the youths, typically met for $1\frac{1}{2}$ hours, five times a week, using a positive peer culture model of group work.

The worker decided to devote one meeting a week to talking about one specific goal each youth had and how each youth was successfully making progress toward the identified goal. Since the worker had 90 minutes for his meeting and eight youths in his group, the worker provided each youth with 10 minutes to talk about the goal and then to answer the question: "How have things been better this week?" Group members provided reflections intended to verify each member's progress. At the end of the meeting, 10 minutes was allocated to reflect on the overall aspects of the group session.

SUMMARY

I'm sure there are many other examples of workers in the helping professions who have developed new ways of working with groups that emphasize a strength-focused or goal-focused approach. I hope the examples described above lead other workers to restructure their efforts in constructive ways.

RATIONALES FOR INTERVENTIONS IN CASE STUDIES

Rationales for (1)

A. This move is intended to accentuate the positive aspects of Jean's relationship with George's mother, so that these experiences will give Jean something to build on.

B. This move uses a presupposition that may strengthen Jean's commitment to talk to George's mother. If Jean accepts this lead, she can focus on how to actually arrange the meeting while she is doing her work now in the group.

C. This move seeks Jean's "here-and-now" goal by asking her to specify how this group can be helpful to her at this time.

D. This move is intended to seek reasons for Jean's lack of communication with George's mother in the past. It may lead Jean to focus on her own inadequacy.

Rationales for (2)

A. This move simply reflects the difficult time George's mother has had in order to elicit some sympathy for her from Jean. This may allow Jean to see the mother's side of things.

B. This move seeks descriptive information from Jean about when she did get along with George's mother, so that she can become more aware of the successful behaviors she may have carried out.

C. The move is intended to do a little mind reading about the beliefs of George's mother, so that Jean might be made aware of this possibility. Attempting to read someone else's mind is a futile activity.

D. This move seeks Jean's past feelings during a positive interactional moment, in order to locate feelings that may reproduce positive interactions in the future. However, feelings are not a resource people can call on whenever they wish.

Rationales for (3)

A. You are reinforcing the change that Jean has reported so that she can move toward what action she wishes to take.
B. You have acknowledged that she was not successful in the past and you have led her toward doing the opposite.
C. You have connected Jean to one initial concern—one she stated, her worry about what drugs are doing to George. You have also led her toward figuring out how to tell George's mother about that worry.
D. This move attempts to lead Jean to think about what she wants to accomplish—what outcome she wants when she tells George's mother about her concern. The move also presupposes that she will act regarding stating her concern to George's mother.

Rationales for (4)

A. This move returns the focus to Jean at this moment, while acknowledging Carol's problem as a future agenda item.
B. Acknowledges Carol's similar situation and leads to a solution-focused discussion regarding Jean's situation.
C. Asks a closed question seeking agreement or disagreement about a specific problem. A dangerous move because agreement would tend to indicate that communication problems with adults have to be accepted rather than improved.
D. Refocuses on Jean by reinforcing how clear her goal is. In addition, requests solutions from group members, thus using them as resources.

Rationales for (5)

A. A cause-seeking question that really advises Jean to give up trying to make the changes that she has clearly indicated she wants to make.
B. Seeks the outcome that may occur if Jean doesn't act, to see if this outcome is understandable to Jean. If it is, Jean may be more motivated to act.
C. This move intends to lead Jean into enacting the situation in which she will actually tell George's mother. If she starts picturing that scene, she may have moved further than just *talking about* taking action.
D. The move is intended to lead Jean into verbalizing her fears, which may tend to diminish their strength.

Rationales for (6)

A. This move emphasizes the here-and-now and uses the group situation to allow Jean to reflect on what she may like or dislike about her approach to George's mother, so that she can either modify the approach or use it as her plan of action.

B. This move leads Jean to the next step. It is really like double-chairing in Gestalt therapy, and it may help Jean anticipate what will actually happen when she talks to George's mother.

C. The purpose of this move is to model giving helpseekers feedback, using group members as a resource regarding what they are considering to achieve the change they want. In this particular group, some members might be very expert regarding what to say or what not to say to a client.

D. This is an example of a move I don't recommend. It judges Jean's effort by speculating on the mother's attitude when she hears it. It is called "mind reading" and usually restricts creativity and hope for change.

Rationales for (7)

A. This move reinforces timely input from one group member and seeks other input, so that Jean can identify any useful points of view of group members.

B. The move refocuses on solutions and empowers Jean to respond to what Bill has said within a solution frame.

C. This move uses a closed question to seek agreement or disagreement from Jean regarding what Bill has said. It is intended to emphasize that Jean is the final judge of what is useful to her.

D. This move asks Bill to explain his reasoning for his position, thus moving away from Jean's opinion while reinforcing Bill's opinion.

Rationales for (8)

A. This move seeks specific ways George hurts his mother rather than accepting Jean's statement that she knows this to be true.

B. This move takes the here-and-now and asks Jean to consider using her own words when she talks to George's mother.

C. This move is judgmental and focuses on the negative aspect of Jean's relationship with George's mother.

D. This move asks about past behavior and will probably lead Jean to feel badly if she hasn't told George's mother. If she has told her, it obviously didn't work because the problem still exists. Please note, it is a closed question seeking a decision.

Rationales for (9)

- A. This move is intended to focus on the here-and-now by asking Jean to identify what has happened so far in the session.
- B. The move reflects the movement away from Jean's goal, so that Jean can take leadership in getting what she wants from the group.
- C. This move attempts to identify the impossible task Carol has led Jean into trying to determine. It is to be hoped that Jean will agree with the closed statement and move back to her goal.
- D. This move confronts Carol in a negative way and is not the best way to move out of this nonproductive channel the group is in. Furthermore, it may alienate Ann for no useful purpose.

Rationales for (10)

- A. This move seeks causes for something Jean didn't do and is likely to lead her to defending her inaction.
- B. This move leads Jean to consider a response by George's mother to a positive statement Jean just made about her. It is intended to move Jean toward using positive comments when she talks to George's mother.
- C. This move builds off the present moment and moves toward the future by presupposing that Jean will talk to the mother and tell her what she was thinking about her when they got along well.
- D. This closed question seeks a decision about a negative feeling (fear) and the influence that feeling had on Jean's decision to say something positive about George's mother. This is a classic cause-and-effect approach. It is basically a waste of time because Jean is talking about when she got along well with George's mother.

5

GOAL-FOCUSED INTERVIEWING WITH FAMILIES

Group work and family therapy have much in common, as each approach has often borrowed from the other. For example, Virginia Satir (1983) used her own version of the "Go Around" described in the preceding chapter. She would ask each family member, including small children:

"What would you like your family to be like?"

or

"Picture what your family would be like if it was the way you want it to be."

Satir emphasized the use of words that produced images, which then produced feelings. Unlike abstract words, she said, such words had energy.

To use Satir's ideas, a helper may elicit initial goal statements with a family by asking everyone at the session the question below (all members are instructed to simply listen to each other without responding).

The question is: "What one thing could you do (that you're not doing) that would make a significant difference in your family's life together?"

After each person has responded, other family members are then asked to reflect on the response of any other family member.

This technique often "jump-starts" a session into finding ideas about making changes, with the ideas coming from the clients in their language.

For example, the Fitch family was seen regularly while their son was incarcerated in a training school. In a session with the mother and father, the following dialogue took place. (In the previous session, both parents had agreed that they had very little communication with each other, or with their son in the past. They both agreed that increasing communication was a family goal.)

Worker: I'd like to ask each of you to think about one thing that you could do, that's not happening now, that would make a significant difference in your marriage.

Wife: Well, he'd have to talk more, open up more.

Worker: And, what would you have to do to have that happen?

Wife: Well, I don't have any trouble telling him what I'm thinking. He's admitted that we should talk more, but that's as far as it goes.

Worker: So what's not happening that might open him up?

Wife: We're not spending time together, at least with no newspaper reading, no TV.

Worker: And what could you do to have that happen?

Wife: Ask him to give me as much time as he spends with the newspaper and the TV.

Worker: Well, I think he heard that request right now. Let me ask you, Dave, what could you do that would make a difference in your marriage?

Husband: Come down out of my room earlier. I work from 8 p.m. to 4 a.m., so we're on a crazy schedule.

Worker: Exactly when would you come down so that things would be different?

Husband: Eleven o'clock in the morning. I could do that 2 or 3 times a week. I usually don't get down till noon, or even later.

Worker: I'd like you to practice that right now. Pretend it's 11:00 a.m. and you've just sat down together. I'll just be an observer.

This brief transcript clearly shows that any technique is subject to many variations. When the wife states what change would make a difference, she cites a behavior of her husband. The worker leads the wife through a series of questions until she finally concludes that she would have to ask for what she wants in a way that still leaves her husband some time on his own. In this way she will be changing; that is, doing something different, so that her husband may change.

The worker had many choices at that juncture, but wanted to move to the husband as quickly as possible. The process of finding something different for the husband to commit to doing took much less time, thus allowing the worker to lead the couple into interacting with each other, rather than with the worker. This is a major goal of goal focused marital and family therapy. It emphasizes using the resources in the room, and getting out of their way when they are moving toward their goal.

The interaction focuses on the husband and the wife having a common goal—to communicate more with each other. The early focus of a goal-focused approach in family therapy is to find a common goal, one that there seems to be a commitment to on the part of each family member.

In another case, with the Madison Family, the transcripts of their videotaped sessions revealed some ways to work with the resources or strengths the family identified.

As you did in the previous chapters, you will be acting as the helper in the transcript provided below. Please write one move you might use, then select one move from the menu provided, and finally, refer to the rationales for each move.

Jim, the 16-year-old son, had been sentenced to a training school for sexually abusing his 7-year-old cousin when he was baby-sitting for his aunt. There had been three family sessions in which Jim has asked his mother, aunt and grandfather for their forgiveness, and they have all said that they forgive him. All three of them were at this fourth session with Jim and two family workers.

In the first excerpt from the fourth family session, Jim revealed that he was sexually abused by his older cousin when Jim was about 12 years old.

Jim: I want to tell you about the time that George, you know, cousin George, he took me into that empty house down from our house, when I was around 12, and he stuck his penis in my anus, he took away my manhood. You (his mother) weren't there for me.

(Jim is crying as he relates this incident; his speech is sporadic and emotional.)

(Jim cont.): So I had to get my manhood back, and I had to get back at you, I had all that pent-up anger, and that caused me to do what I did to Lisa (his cousin).

Mother: At that time I was drinking most of the time, to deal with all the pressure on me. Your daddy left us, and there was no money, just pressure, pressure. And my drinking led to me neglecting you. I wasn't there for you.

Grandfather: It's good to get all of this out. We're a very strong family, and we can get through this if we get everything out.

Mother: That's right. It's no good holding it in. When I go to AA, I get everything out, so I don't have to drink.

Jim: It's still hard for me to look at Jeanette (his Aunt), 'cause of what I did to her daughter.

Aunt: I want you to know that I forgive you, Jimmy. We're all looking forward to your coming home. Lisa and Marie (younger sister) aren't afraid of you.

They ask all the time, "When is Jimmy coming home?" We all want to be together again.

Worker: Well, one thing everyone seems to agree about is in talking things out. Seems like you're all taking responsibility for the future of the family.

Grandfather: That's right. And they're getting things out now. The big thing is, will Jimmy be accepted when he comes home?

Jim: Yeah! I want to talk about being trusted again.

Mother: I know you can't come home with Daddy and me. We don't have any room in Daddy's place for anyone but us.

(Jim's three siblings have been placed in foster care, and his mother and stepfather have moved into a tiny apartment.)

Worker: As we discussed at our family session last week, Jim has called his grandmother, and she is willing to take him into their home. She wants everyone to be safe, so things can stay calm.

Tim: At least Grandma and Granddad trust me.

You: (1)_____ _____

_____

_____

Now look at the four answers below. In addition to checking an answer, you will now be asked to write your own rationale for the answer you chose.

Please check one of the choices below.

Answers for (1):

A. ___ What could family members say to you, Jim, that would help you feel more trusted?

B. ___ How do each of you feel about Grandma's idea of keeping everyone safe?

C. ___ You are responsible for losing some trust, Jim.

D. ___ How do you feel about not being trusted, Jim?

Now write a rationale below for the choice you selected.

_____

_____

_____

Now turn to page 65 to read rationales for each answer above. Then continue reading the script. You will be the worker:

You: What could family members say to you, Jim, that would help you feel more trusted?

Jeanette: Well, we do stick together as a family.

You: Well, that's certainly true. And you've shown a remarkable change since Jim first came here. Instead of avoiding problems, you now face up to them.

Jeanette: That's what people have to do.

You: And I want to face one. I want to face an absolute need. I want to support Grandma's idea of safety. Jeanette's daughters can never be unsafe again.

Jim: So you're saying I can't be trusted to sit for Jeanette's kids again.

You: (2)_____

_____

_____

Please check one of the choices below.

Answers for (2):

    A. ____ Yes, I am. At least, not by yourself.

    B. ____ No, I don't think you should feel that way.

    C. ____ You don't want to get back in trouble again, do you?

    D. ____ I'm saying that the family has to guarantee that Jeanette's daughters will be safe in the future, and that you will be safe from ever being put in jail again.

Now write a rationale below for the choice you selected.

_____

_____

_____

Now turn to page 65 to read rationales for each answer above. Then continue reading the script.

You: I'm saying that the family has to guarantee that Jeanette's daughters will be safe in the future, and that you will be safe from ever being put in jail again.

Jim: I don't see how my safety is part of sitting the kids.

You: Who in the family can help Jim understand that?

Jeanette: Well, I know my daughters. When they have a sitter now, they act kinda weird. You know, silly, and kinda bad.

You: What do you think they would be like with Jim?

Jeanette: Well, they don't talk like they're afraid of Jimmy, but they do think that he might be afraid of them. They even giggle when they talk about him sitting.

You: (3) _____

_____

_____

Please check one of the choices below.

Answers for (3):

A. ___ So they think they could get away with things when Jim was sitting?

B. ___ What do they mean when they say Jim's afraid?

C. ___ What do you think they are giggling about?

D. ___ How do you feel about them giggling about your sitting, Jim?

Now write a rationale below for the choice you selected.

_____

_____

_____

Now turn to pages 65 and 66 to read rationales for each answer above. Then continue reading the script.

You: What do you think they are giggling about?

Jeanette: Well, they kinda have power over Jimmy. Like he got in big trouble for messing with them.

You: So what does that past stuff have to do with the family in the future?

Mom: Well, we want to all get back together again and live without that pressure we had. We're really got to take care of each other, so like you said, the kids are safe.

You: And Jim too. He can't ever be sent to a prison again.

Mom: That's for sure. I can't go through this nightmare again.

You: (4) _____

_____

_____

Please check one of the choices below.

Answers for (4):

    A. ___ What is helping you get to daylight now?

    B. ___ It must have been hard on you.

    C. ___ And that's the reason to prevent future problems.

    D. ___ Tell us more about the nightmare.

Now write a rationale below for the choice you selected.

_____

_____

_____

Now turn to page 66 to read rationales for each answer above. Then continue reading the script.

You: What is helping you get to daylight now?

Mom: Thinking about the future, and about good things.

Jim: It's been hard for me too.

Mom: Yes, that's for sure. You're in here thinking about the bad things. But that's behind us, and going to Grandma's will give everyone a fresh start.

Grandpa: We're looking forward to Jim coming with us, and even more to the family all getting together.

You: And we think Jim's ready to successfully make it with your careful planning. You have all worked hard in family sessions to deal with the problems the family was having.

Mom: We weren't having any more than most families.

You: (5) _____

_____

_____

Please check one of the choices below.

Answers for (5):

    A. ___ Most families do have quite a few problems.

    B. ___ Most families don't have a child put in a training school.

    C. ___ That seems to be a very defensive statement.

    D. ___ I'm glad you feel that way. Otherwise you wouldn't be coping as well as you are.

Now write a rationale below for the choice you selected.

_____

_____

_____

Now turn to page 66 to read rationales for each answer above. Then continue reading the script.

You: I'm glad you feel that way. Otherwise you wouldn't be coping as well as you are.

Mom: We're better off now than we were. I am, with less pressure.

You: The pressure is reduced now?

Mom: Oh, in every way.

You: What do you mean?

Mom: I'm getting help, with the kids, with finding a house. I never got help before. (Note: The children have been placed in foster care.)

You: (6) _____

_____

_____

Please check one of the choices below.

Answers for (6):

A. ___ And you've reached out for that help, and you're really using that help effectively.

B. ___ That's probably why you have changed so much—from keeping things in to really facing up to them.

C. ___ And with that help, how do you feel you've changed?

D. ___ You're really facing things now that you used to avoid. What can you do so you can avoid having that pressure come back?

Now write a rationale below for the choice you selected.

_____

_____

_____

Now turn to page 66 to read rationales for each answer above. Then continue reading the script.

You: And you've reached out for that help, and you're really using that help effectively.

Jeanette: And I'm getting help with my kids, and Jim's getting help. The parenting classes are a big help, and these meetings are helping Jim.

You: How will this help affect the future?

Jeanette: We've got a long way to go to get our lives in shape. Too much to bear... at least alone, in the past.

Jim: I think when they saw I was changing, from the stuff I was working on, then they wanted to use help too.

You: What do the rest of you think of what Jim is saying?

Mom: Well, getting things out has really helped. We feel the difference.

You: (7) _____

_____

Please check your preferred choice below.

Answers for (7):

A. ___ What difference do you mean?

B. ___ Why have you changed?

C. ___ What is needed to keep the changes you've made?

D. ___ And it will be hard to avoid slipping back to the old patterns.

Now write a rationale below for the choice you selected.

_____

_____

Now turn to page 67 to read rationales for each answer above. Then continue reading the script.

You: What is needed to keep the changes you've made?

Jeanette: We can't just talk. We have to plan...

Mom: Oh, we're really different as a family. We talk with each other just like we do here with you. And we never did that before.

You: Well, you have sure opened up to each other here. That's important for a family to do pretty regularly. What were you starting to say, Jeanette?

Jeanette: I was talking about planning things. We never did much of that.

You: I was thinking the same thing.

Jeanette: We've got to plan so the family doesn't have more trouble like this.

You: (8) _____

_____

_____

Please check your preferred choice below.

Answers for (8):

A. ___ Do you agree with Jeanette, Mom, regarding the need to plan?

B. ___ Try to do a little planning right now.

C. ___ I'd like to suggest two kinds of planning. Jim needs to plan with both Grandpa and Grandma; and Mom, you and Joe need to plan for the return of all the kids.

D. ___ How come you've never done planning in the past?

Now write a rationale below for the choice you selected.

_____

_____

_____

Now turn to page 67 to read rationales for each answer above. Then continue reading the script.

You: I'd like to suggest two kinds of planning. Jim needs to plan with both Grandpa and Grandma; and Mom, you and Joe need to plan for the return of all the kids.

Mom: I'm not worried about getting the kids back too soon, since we need to find a house first.

You: That is an important job. And finding where to get help in getting the house.

Mom: Yeah, we've started to work with social services, but we need more help to get things moving.

You: (9) _____

_____

_____

Please check your preferred response below.

Answers for (9):

   A. ___ What have you tried so far?
   B. ___ What's holding up things regarding getting a house?
   C. ___ Do you have enough money for a house?
   D. ___ There probably aren't any houses you can afford.

Now write a rationale below for the choice you selected.

_____

_____

_____

Now turn to page 67 to read rationales for each answer above. Then continue reading the script.

You: What's holding up things regarding getting a house?

Mom: Social Services is supposed to help us, but you can get to feel left out there.

Jim: Seems like I'm left out right now.

You: What do you see yourself doing in relation to what the family is talking about?

Jim: Talking with Grandma about coming to her house.

You: Grandpa, can you involve Jim in this discussion?

Grandpa: Well, I don't know.

You: (10)_____

_____

_____

Please check your preferred response below.

Answers for (10):

   A. ___ Can you take the first step in meeting with Grandma and Jim?
   B. ___ What about you, Mom?
   C. ___ Let's finish the planning Mom needs to do, and then look at you and Grandpa.
   D. ___ You usually have good ideas about the key issue.

Now write a rationale below for the choice you selected.

_____

_____

_____

Now turn to pages 67 and 68 to read rationales for each answer above.

RATIONALS FOR INTERVENTIONS IN CASE STUDIES

Rationales for (1)

A. This is an inaccurate response. Jim's statement implies that other family members do not trust him (i.e., mother, aunt).

B. This is the preferred move, in that it asks Jim what people would have to give him in order to increase his trust. The goal here is an increase, not a total level of trust.

C. This is a poor move which blames Jim for this lack of trust. You don't get people to accept responsibility for their past acts through attempting to induce guilt.

D. This move emphasizes the hole instead of the doughnut. Jim is trusted by his grandparents, and the transcript certainly shows high levels of trust from his aunt.

Rationales for (2)

A. This is a clear, accurate statement that deals with safety for everyone, and particularly the two young girls.

B. This statement argues with Jim, and ignores the safety of Jeanette's children.

C. This closed question offers no opportunity for movement, since it is rhetorical in form.

D. This is the preferred move, in that it states a potential goal for the entire family, and one that matches their past words about safety.

Rationales for (3)

A. This is a leading move, attempting to clarify what the giggling might mean in a way that would support Jim not sitting with the girls as being in his own best interest.

B. This is a simple request for Jeanette to clarify the meaning of what she is saying, so that she and other family members might better understand this perspective. Hopefully, they will use the viewpoint to ensure everyone's safety.

C. Similar to (b), in that it requests a clarification of meaning for all the same purposes as (b).

D. This move attempts to elicit feelings that will likely be negative and not useful in producing movement in designing the actions that will tend to prevent Jim's future placement in prison.

Rationales for (4)

A. This preferred move transforms the mother's word "nightmare" and focuses on what strengths are helping her with her life right now.

B. This move is clearly empathetic, but focuses on the past "nightmare," and is likely to elicit more problem-talking about the past.

C. This closed statement may actually lead to avoiding talk about the problems of the past by moving to a future focus.

D. This very poor move clearly asks for a problem-saturation story.

Rationales for (5)

A. This move normalizes the family's situation in order to join the mother's view of the families in general.

B. A very confrontational move that puts the mother down, as opposed to respecting her.

C. Labeling the mother's statement without addressing her intent; that is, to defend and stand up for her own family.

D. Matching the mother's strength regarding her own family, and reinforcing her actions in dealing with the difficulties the family is experiencing.

Rationales for (6)

A. Reinforces differences in seeking and using both external and internal resources.

B. Emphasizes the new way the mother and the family are overcoming their difficulties.

C. Elicits a personal change story, in order to solidify the changes.

D. Reinforces changes that have occurred and asks for actions that will maintain the changes.

(All these moves are appropriate.)

Rationales for (7)

A. A simple clarification of the mother's use of a key word, so that changes she has seen will be heard by other family members, and reinforced for herself through saying them.

B. A possible positive use of the question "why?," since seeking reasons for desirable changes can lead to identifying positive resources or strengths upon which to build.

C. This question jumps a little too far ahead, since the changes or differences the mother is thinking about have not been put into visual terms that will provide energy or motivation for achieving family goals.

D. A basic restraint-from-change move, in that it emphasizes how hard it is to maintain change, and makes it normal if some relapse does occur.

Rationales for (8)

A. A good closed question, which seeks to find agreement between the sisters, and a commitment to planning, if the mother says "Yes."

B. A leading move using the opportunity, here and now, to build off Jeanette's commitment to planning.

C. A leading move toward designing two different plans of action to deal with two different environments which may eventually help unify this family.

D. An obviously poor move, placing the family in a one-down position of defending their past behavior.

Rationales for (9)

A. A commonly used move that tends to elicit failures, or excuses, for not making any effort.

B. This move seeks to identify obstacles to getting a house, so that ways to overcome the obstacles can be developed by designing appropriate actions.

C. A closed personal question that serves no useful purpose in helping the family achieve its goals.

D. An obviously judgmental statement that has no place in a therapeutic interaction.

Rationales for (10)

A. The worker has allowed Jim to change the topic under discussion, and left mom up in the air. Planning Jim's placement with his grandparents will best be handled after a plan is in place to help the mother find a house where the family can be reunited.

B. Connecting Mom to the issue of Jim going to the grandmother's home doesn't seem to make much sense.

C. This is the preferred move. Jim has cut off the house-finding discussion, as well as his mother. Completing this theme is strongly related to the family's goal of becoming unified.

D. Bringing Grandpa in regarding the current theme is not necessary, since he is not (seemingly) a resource for this set of actions.

SUMMARY

The Madison Family case, with the menus and the rationales provided, emphasizes the following principles about using goal-focused interviewing with families:

1. Find goals for all individuals and the family as a whole.
2. Emphasize family strengths, particularly each member's internal resources.
3. Find external resources.
4. Encourage family member-to-member interaction about their goals, strengths, and resources.
5. Listen for positive differences that have occurred and reinforce any differences that relate to the desired outcomes (goals).

(For the purpose of this book, only small parts of a total family session can be used. Clearly, the issue of Jim's sexual abuse was left without any closure, since the family members led the discussion to their issues. The family returned to this issue later in the session and over the next two sessions.)

6

ORGANIZING INFORMATION

Many schemes intend to visualize the information being shared in a therapy session, such as family mapping, ecograms, genograms, and field diagrams. None of these designs helps show an interviewing process in dynamic form. To find a diagramming process that would fit GFI, I have borrowed from the force field concepts that have been used primarily to describe organizations. The version described below has been tested with more than 25 client systems. Clients responded positively in general and several asked for a copy.

The two major ingredients of the force field approach that appealed to me are the identification of the two extremes for any client situation. On the left side of the diagram, the worst case scenario is identified, and on the right side, the ideal state is described. The present situation is represented by a line somewhere between the two extremes.

The process of clarifying these two extreme scenarios with clients is very useful because the worst case scenario is usually much worse than the person's present problem situation. In addition, the ideal state, though unlikely to ever be totally realized, pushes past the limitations people tend to put on themselves when they try to talk about what is "realistic."

The design of a force field emphasizes a dynamic picture of the client's immediate situation, as shown in the following diagram.

Force Field

| Worst case scenario | Forces pulling toward the worst case scenario | Forces pulling toward the desired state | Desired state |

NOTE: After several trials in social work methods classes, I reversed the normal direction of the arrows in a force field, thus changing from forces that pushed against the middle line to forces that pulled or led the middle line in one direction or another.

As stated above, the line in the middle of the diagram depicts where the client system is at the present time. In the case presented in this chapter, an initial force field was developed in the first 10 minutes of the interview.

CASE STUDY 6

Larry, a substance-abusing client, was working with a therapist to deal with his recent relapse. This was Larry's third relapse since a 30-day hospitalization. His early interaction with his therapist is shown in the transcript following the force field below, so that you can see how the force field diagram was developed.

Force Field I

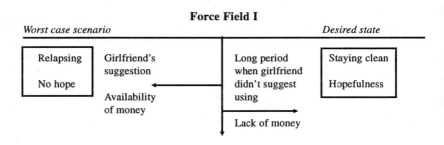

The first interactions of the therapy session are provided in the following dialogue.

Larry: I was sitting with my girlfriend (they have lived together for 8 years) and she suddenly suggested I go get some crack.

Therapist: You seem surprised that she made such a suggestion.

Larry: It's the first time she ever has. I've lost my job over my hospitalization, so we spend a lot more time together and maybe we were just bored.

Therapist: Where did you get the money to buy it?

Larry: That's the unbelievable part. I sold my truck for $150 to get the money.

Therapist: And your truck was worth. . . .

Larry: At least $5,000. I got to get it back.

Now look back at Force Field I and try to add some additional forces to those presented in the diagram. They will be identified in Force Field II below.

As the interview continued, additional forces were identified, goals or problems were clarified, and previously identified forces were stated in more accurate ways. Questions were asked in such a way as to elicit strengths, partially successful efforts in the past, or unique outcomes demonstrating when the client was able to handle the problem.

Therapist: So how long have you been going between relapses?

Larry: A month or more. I used to use the stuff every week.

Therapist: What do you think will help you extend the time to even more than a month?

Larry: Well, therapy for one thing. Therapy with you gives me a lift. I know you care about me and about me getting clean. So regular individual therapy would help.

Therapist: And what else would help?

Larry: I don't know what it will take.

Therapist: Maybe avoiding people that get you to use.

Larry: Oh, I'm not giving up Betsy. She's all I've got. I'm cut off from my kids, except for 3-day visits twice a year, and my mother and father are both drunks. I don't see them at all. Funny, I swore I'd never drink because of the way they are, but I found something worse.

Therapist: Sounds pretty hopeless.

Larry: Well, I've lost a lot of things. Even the job I had for 9 years. Only thing I ever did well for a length of time like that. But I'm tired of the way things are now. I can't take it any longer.

Using the material above, the following force field was drawn up.

Force Field II

Worst case scenario	Forces pulling toward relapse	Forces pulling toward staying clean	Desired state
Relapse	"Extra" money Power of crack addiction No money for therapy Cut off from children Loss of job	Lack of money for dope Seeking therapy Girlfriend's support over 8 years Degree of desperation "I can't take it any longer" Decreasing use of crack Keeping a job for 9 years	Staying clean

As stated earlier, the vertical line depicts the present distance between the worst case scenario and the desired state. The goal of therapy is to move the line toward the righthand side. The following are ways to enhance the likelihood of this occurrence:

1. Increase the positive forces in intensity.
2. Find new forces (resources, strengths).
3. Decrease strength of negative forces.
4. Eliminate a negative force.

One way to develop an action design that tends to move the line to the right is to focus on the future by having interactions with Larry that emphasize his strengths and his way of looking at the future. This is pictured in the next diagram (Force Field III).

Force Field III emerged when the therapist explored Larry's resources (accounting, above-average intelligence, internal strengths to go a month without crack). Larry reduced the influence of the past by reducing his problem-saturated talking, and sought an uncle who was a banker so that he could send his unemployment checks to him.

Force Field III: The Future

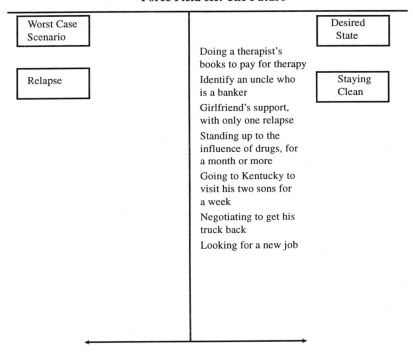

The long list of positive forces cited in Force Field III are essential to break a crack addiction, as Larry is well aware. The changing of his belief of hopelessness to one of being challenged to overcome the odds against him was the primary reason for "covering all bases" in the future force field. In addition, the diagram itself became Larry's action plan, and he took a copy with him when he left the session.

Now I'd like to give you a chance to practice the force field technique. We'll use the Madison family from Chapter 5 as the client system to be diagrammed. Please reread pages 60 through 71, and then fill out the force field below. I have provided some labels for the worst case scenario and the desired outcome.

Force Field IV

Worst Case Scenario		Desired Outcome
Abuse or neglect		United and safe

Now compare your diagram with the one provided. Your diagram should look somewhat like the one below.

Force Field V

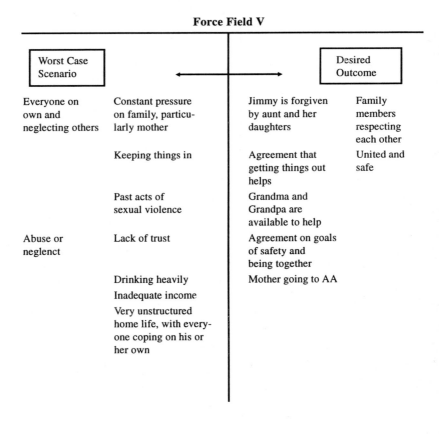

Worst Case Scenario			Desired Outcome	
Everyone on own and neglecting others	Constant pressure on family, particularly mother		Jimmy is forgiven by aunt and her daughters	Family members respecting each other
	Keeping things in		Agreement that getting things out helps	United and safe
	Past acts of sexual violence		Grandma and Grandpa are available to help	
Abuse or neglenct	Lack of trust		Agreement on goals of safety and being together	
	Drinking heavily		Mother going to AA	
	Inadequate income			
	Very unstructured home life, with everyone coping on his or her own			

After the force field has been completed, it can be used to design an action plan. The targets of change will involve increasing the forces on the right side of the diagram and adding new positive forces, or decreasing the negative forces on the left side.

Now, please read pages 60 through 66 to see what the worker actually started to do as the focus moved to the future for the family. Then fill out the future force field below.

Force Field VI

Worst Case Scenario		Desired Outcome

Very
unstructured
family life

United
and
safe

Now compare your force field with the one below.

Force Field VII

Worst Case Scenario			Desired Outcome
	Possible resumption of drinking	Reduced pressure with kids placed in foster care	
Very unstructured family life	Possible increased economic pressure on family	Continuing with AA; family's commitment to Responsibly planning future family life	United and safe
	Red tape involved in getting a house through DSS	Changes Jim sees in himself and family sees in him through help	
	Loss of therapy when Jim leaves training school	Willingness to accept and use help, such as parenting skills, finding a house	
	Relapse into holding things in	Continuing to talk openly with each other— get things out	
		Seeing differences in each other, in the family as a whole	
		Grandparents ready to take Jim	
		Family therapy picked up by follow-up worker in community who attends the last meetings in the closed setting	

As you can clearly see, a future-focused force field evolves by diminishing negative forces or by transforming them into positive forces. For example, when the family therapy is picked up by a community worker, this balances the loss of therapy available in the training school. Though this service is available, the therapist will need to invite the community worker to the last family meetings to enhance continuity.

As in the first example in this chapter, this case includes many powerful negative forces that require multiple efforts to overcome. The eight positive forces will be prioritized as part of the action planning, but it will probably be necessary to activate all of them in order to continue the momentum the family has achieved in moving toward change.

POTENTIAL USES OF THE FORCE FIELD

To publicly maintain a record of the information being shared, a worker can use a newsprint pad to write out a force field while working with a family. The client system can take a copy with them as a reminder of their session and of the commitments they made.

The information in the force field can also be used by workers who intend to write reflective letters to clients between sessions. At least some of the positive forces would be included in a letter to the client system.

Finally, the force field can be included in the case record and updated regularly. It offers much more dynamic information than the typical abstract labeling included in many client files.

The Madison family case offers you a good opportunity to practice writing a reflective letter to a family and then to compare it with the one provided. Use the space below to write your own letter, and then compare it with the one on the following page.

YOUR REFLECTIVE LETTER

EXAMPLE OF A LETTER TO THE MADISON FAMILY

I am writing to make sure you know how impressed I have been with the strength of your family. You are unique in your commitment to a large number of family meetings, and even more unique in having four of them videotaped.

You have clearly forgiven Jim for his actions against his cousins, and your forgiveness is one of the strongest forces toward bringing the family back together. Not many families have three generations all pulling together to unite their family in a safe environment.

You have talked often of the importance of being open with each other and how different that is from the way you kept things within you in the past. You have also faced the neglect of the past and how the use of alcohol may have led to that. You are very motivated to actions: to getting a house, to safety for everyone, to planning the family's future, and I think your planning will be carried out and will take you all to daylight.

Sincerely,

SUMMARY

This chapter has described a method that visualizes critical information for all participants in therapy through the use of force field diagrams on newsprint pads. In addition, the force field method can be used in client files, so that any agency worker can quickly see the client system's difficulties and strengths. The force field provides a context for both the difficulties and the strengths of the client system, thus giving life to the information gathered.

Finally, the force field provides the material for a reflective letter by citing the key information in outline form.

7

THE SILENT INTERVIEW

A common question from social work students is, What do you do when a client won't answer any of your questions?

The response from many theoretical approaches to a refusal to talk, or any form of resistance, is to join the resistance. Using the principals of GFI, this means matching the client. To match perfectly, the worker can ask the client to remain silent, keeping all information within. The worker, using primarily closed questions or directives, asks the client to simply nod or shake his or her head in answer to each question. Permission to answer yes or no is also given.

The helper then guides the client through the GFI process. The helper starts by asking the client to focus on one area of life in which some difficulty is occurring, or one thing he or she'd like to change about himself or herself, or about a relationship with which he or she is struggling.

The next step is to ask the client to visualize the situation when the problem has been solved. When the client indicates, with a head nod, that he or she has this picture, the client has identified the desired state.

The helper then leads the client to think about resources and strengths that can be used in a designed action plan for achieving the desired state. It is important to note that the obstacles become the problem that must be overcome.

CAST STUDY 7

The following script describes how to open a silent interview (based on over 30 interviews I've conducted).

Helper: What we're going to try out here is called a silent interview. I'll do all the talking, while you listen and either agree with a question by nodding your head, or disagree by shaking your head. You can also say yes or no, if you wish. Am I clear so far?

Wendy: Yes.

Helper: Okay. This type of interview is based on the belief that you already have the information you need to change something that's bothering you, and my job is to lead your thinking to find the most useful information. Think about what you were focusing on when you volunteered for this demonstration, and nod your head when you're picturing that troubling situation.

Wendy: (Nods head three times)

After these directions, the worker leads the client through an 8- or 10-minute interview, which will be described below. Following the interview, the worker leads the client through a very important debriefing process, with the client freely talking about how he or she experienced the entire silent interview. No information is shared about the problem, although clients often insist on talking about their action design or their action priorities.

In many debriefings, clients have consistently emphasized how focused the interview was, and how rapidly they could find solutions within themselves when they didn't have to think of the words they were willing to share with the helper.

One client said, "In every therapy session, I spend most of my energy trying to think of how I can explain my problems to my therapist so that she will understand. In this approach, it's like watching a silent movie, with me acting in the ways that I usually just talk about."

Obviously a silent interview is the least intrusive form of helping, and provides the highest respect for the capacity of clients to deal with their own problems, draw on their own strengths, find new resources, and design their own plan to achieve their goals.

This approach also allows the helper to focus on the client's nonverbal communication, as there is no need to attempt to listen to and understand verbal content. The helper can concentrate on distinguishing between a hesitant "yes" and a very firm, high-volume "yes!" The helper can also carefully track the client's eye scan patterns, using the guide from my previous book, *Dynamic Interviewing*. A brief, simplified description of eye scan patterns includes

Nonverbal cues	Interpretation
eyes looking upward	visualizing
eyes unfocused	visualizing
eyes sideways	recalling auditory words or sounds
eyes down	experiencing kinesthetic sensations

In addition to the data provided by the client's eye scan patterns, facial expressions can be easily noted, such as smiles and frowns. All this data allow the helper to make decisions about the direction the interview is taking. The flow chart below is provided to remind you of the basic steps in a goal-focused interview.

Note: It is important to point out that every interview doesn't involve all these steps, or always in the same sequence. For instance, many clients will state their problem *and* their goal in their opening statement. Further, the obstacle frame and the resource frame are often reversed because the client often identifies obstacles that prevent the use of a resource.

Flow Chart for a Goal-Focused Interview

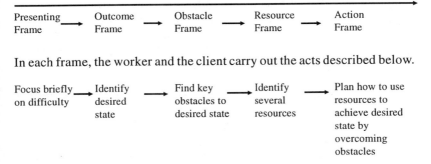

In each frame, the worker and the client carry out the acts described below.

Presenting Frame →	Outcome Frame →	Obstacle Frame →	Resource Frame →	Action Frame
Focus briefly on difficulty →	Identify desired state →	Find key obstacles to desired state →	Identify several resources →	Plan how to use resources to achieve desired state by overcoming obstacles

HOW TO CONDUCT A SILENT INTERVIEW

The specific steps that follow are a guide to conducting a silent interview. Workers should modify the questions and even the sequence of questions in any way that emphasizes ongoing movement during the interview. One delightful occurrence in many silent interviews is when the client asks permission to talk. Of course, such permission is immediately given. (Note: For purposes of brevity, the client throughout the steps will be referred to as "she.")

Step 1: Ask the client to think about something she would like to change in her life, and to nod her head when she finds something.

Step 2: Ask, "Is it important to you to change the situation you're thinking of?"

(If yes, go to step 3; if no, return to step 1)

Step 3: "When the situation has been changed, picture what you will be like, and nod your head when you have that picture."

(It is important to move slowly here, waiting patiently for the head nod. If the client doesn't nod her head, you can ask alternative questions, such as:)

What will you be doing?
How will you be different?

(If she can't find a picture, it is best to return to step 1.)

Note: When clients can picture themselves doing their goal behavior, it moves them from hope to possibilities. When they can't, your work involves asking a client for examples of people who do the things they want to be doing. For example, a couple in a verbal interview wanted to communicate better with each other. When asked for a time when they did communicate well, they agreed "never." When asked who they knew that communicated the way they wanted, they said all their friends had this problem. The worker then found a TV show that was an example of the way they wanted to communicate (Rosanne and her husband Dan).

Step 4: "Now think about what is holding you up from being the way you want to be."
Alternative directive: "Preventing you from doing what you want to be doing."

Step 5: "Please nod your head when you've found something that is holding you up, like an obstacle that constrains you."

Step 6: "Now think of a person who could help you to get past this obstacle."

(When there is a head nod, place the person in the situation in which change is desired.)

Step 7: "Is this person involved in the situation you want to change?"

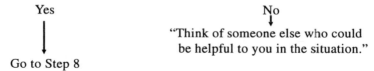

Yes

Go to Step 8

No

"Think of someone else who could be helpful to you in the situation."

Step 8: The worker now says something like: "It's wonderful to have people in the living situation who can help you change that situation. Picture yourself talking to that person. Tell the person how you want things to be different in that environment."

Then say, "Nod your head when you can picture talking to that person."

Step 9: Watch the person's responses to your messages.

(Worker will watch client's facial expressions and accurately reflect them to client.)

    A. "You're smiling. Does that mean it went well?"
    B. "You're frowning. You're having trouble involving your friend in your solution."
    C. (If B is true, ask: "Would you like to try it again? Think of how you could change the situation so it might go better, and nod your head when you've had a little success.")

(Note: If seeking external resources does not provide the client with a support, or inadequate support to achieve the desired outcome, you will want to move to internal resources by asking about those times when the client has found the internal strength to deal with a similar "stuck" situation. Remember, you are seeking strengths that will break the client out of the holding, or "stuck," pattern, so that movement toward the desired outcome occurs.)

Step 10: To access internal resources, give a directive, such as: "Please go inside and find a part of you that helps you keep going in tough situations, and nod your head when you've found one."

Step 11: Give the client plenty of time to find a resource. If the client can't find one, cue the client by saying something like:

Probes: "Maybe it's a phrase you say to yourself."

"Maybe it's a visual picture of yourself doing something well, as in a sport or game."

Step 12: "Ask that part of you if it will help you get moving toward your goal, and nod your head if it says yes."

If the client nods, ask for a second internal resource, or a way of functioning that has helped him or her move forward in the past (e.g., deep breathing, muscle relaxing, muscle tightening and releasing, etc.)

If the client shakes her head indicating *no,* say, "I think I have rushed you. Let's go slower and seek your internal strengths again."

Step 13: If the client still can't think of an internal resource, share any resources that have been helpful to you, such as deep breathing.

Step 14: After finding one or two internal resources, ask the client to place herself back in the situation in which she seems stuck. Ask her to see her friend, and then activate her internal resources and watch the scene unfold.

Step 15: Ask the client to note the differences in the scene now as compared with the past. Say, "Watch yourself in particular to see yourself functioning in a different way, in a competent way. Nod your head when you see this competent behavior."

Step 16: Again, as in Step 9, watch the client's nonverbal cues and reflect to her what you see. Allow the client to pace herself. If she can't see herself functioning more competently, go back to any necessary step from 7 on.

Because the client is entirely in charge of any progress in a silent interview, you may also find that she shakes her head most of the time, indicating little or no progress has been achieved. You may then move to helping the client accept the situation she finds herself in, and acceptance becomes the goal of the interview.

A silent interview offers workers tremendous opportunities to build on the responses of clients. When no words are stated, progress toward the goal can be easily identified, in the nonverbal responses of the client. In this way, less time is spent exploring dead ends or problem-saturated stories.

As for the client, she can devote her energy toward finding another side, or multiple sides, of her inner self. As a client accesses these different selves, she may see her situation from a different perspective or find useful beliefs far different from those that have controlled her functioning in the past.

8

OTHER USES OF GOAL-FOCUSED INTERVIEWING

Goal-focused Interviewing has been used as an indirect means of treatment in several ways:

1. For single-session consultation interviews with significant persons in the client's system (i.e., teachers, family members not in the primary treatment sessions, and bosses).
2. When meeting with other service providers in the helping profession.
3. In case consultation sessions involving staff groups.
4. As a model for elementary and secondary school teachers to use in parent-teacher conferences.

Each of these uses will be described in this chapter.

CONSULTING WITH THE CLIENT SYSTEM USING GFI

In many instances, you can use this goal-focused method when consulting with the significant people in a client's system. Of necessity, such consultation is quite brief, and it is essential that it conclude with a clear plan and priorities for implementing that plan spelled out in writing. Using reflective letters in such a situation can significantly increase the coordination of the entire system in implementing the plan.

In the following case, the helper was working with the mother of a family but found that the focus of the problem was between the child and his teacher. The material below includes brief interactions between the mother and the helper and then a script of the helper-teacher interaction.

CASE STUDY 8

A mother was concerned about her 10-year-old son's lack of progress in school, and about his immature behavior at home. Tim is an only child, with a very distant father, a doctor, who is seldom home.

The mother stated that she had to do everything for Tim, even putting his milk on his cereal in the morning. She had to prod him to go to school each day and make sure he didn't forget his books or school supplies.

The mother had gone to the school seeking help, and a plan had been developed for "organizing" Tim. A notebook had been started to keep track of his assignments, but he frequently "forgot" to bring it home and finally "lost" it.

When the helper asked what the mother wanted things to be like, she said, "I'd like my son to do better in school, so I can get those teachers off my back."

The mother and the helper designed an action plan, with the first priority being a visit by the helper to Tim's school to meet with the teacher. The mother felt she became too emotional when she went to the school, so that nothing happened that led to any kind of change.

The transcript below describes the meeting with the helper and Mrs. Shaw, Tim's teacher.

Mrs. Shaw started the interview by blurting out:

Mrs. Shaw: Tim's the worst student in the fourth grade. All the teachers talk about the difficulties they've had with him, even as far back as first grade. He's behind all other students in math and reading and he now refuses to do any work.

Helper: What work do you want him to do, in particular?

Mrs. Shaw: Mainly desk work, when each student has an individual assignment to finish in 20 or 25 minutes.

Helper: I'm sure you're giving him work he can handle.

Mrs. Shaw: Yes, in fact, we've specifically designed materials that we're sure he can easily do.

Helper: So you'd be satisfied if he completed the work you give him during this 20- to 25-minute period of desk work.

Mrs. Shaw: I'd be satisfied if he did half of it. The teachers talk about him all the time. His third grade teacher passed him on to get rid of him, and she admits it.

Helper: When a kid like this frustrates so many teachers, he's usually enjoying doing that. Do you think he's enjoying having this power over all of you?

Mrs. Shaw: Oh, I'm sure of it. We've tried to get him organized by giving him a notebook with all his work, but he always loses it.

Helper: And then what happens?

Mrs. Shaw: Then we have to start all over again and get a new notebook with all his assignments. And I have to nag him to get him to do the little he does do.

Helper: So how do you want things to be different from they have been in the past?

Mrs. Shaw: I want Tim to work independently, without all the prodding and nagging and organizing we have been doing. (Mrs. Shaw has a teacher's aide).

Helper: When do you want him to this independent work?

Mrs. Shaw: Well, we have desk work time three times a day, and that's the time I'm thinking of.

Helper: And when he is working independently, give me a picture of what you and your aide will be doing.

Mrs. Shaw: That's the really hard part. It's so difficult to ignore him when I know he isn't doing a thing.

Helper: And what's happened when you didn't ignore him in the past?

Mrs. Shaw: I've gone over and prodded him . . . tried to get him started.

Helper: And what happened?

Mrs. Shaw: He did little or nothing.

Helper: So what have you got to lose by ignoring him?

Mrs. Shaw: Well, when I prod him, at least I feel like I'm doing something.

Helper: So with this new plan, instead of prodding Tim, what will you and your aide be doing?

Mrs. Shaw: We can do some of our class planning together quietly, over in our work area.

Helper: How likely is it that you'll be able to ignore Tim?

Mrs. Shaw: Oh, I think we can, for at least two or three weeks.

Helper: You sound very strong, the way you say that. I'm amazed about how long you expect to be successful in ignoring Tim.

Mrs. Shaw: Well, we've tried everything else, and like you said, he's getting a kick out of running us around.

Helper: Well, fine. Please let me know how it works. I'll call you in a week to find out.

In the follow-up phone call, Mrs. Shaw reported that Tim did absolutely nothing for two days. From the third day to the tenth day he completed all or most of his work, and he "found" the missing notebook and used it to keep track of his assignments.

As this case shows, Mrs. Shaw found that the major obstacle was within herself, as she had to see that ignoring Tim was actually doing something, and something different from what she had tried in the past. In addition, she identified a different goal—Tim working independently—rather than "getting him to do something."

CASE STUDY 9:
CONSULTING WITH OTHER HELPERS

A worker came to me with a videotape of a session he had with a father, mother, and their 17-year-old son who was incarcerated in a training school. The worker was feeling very successful in achieving one of the family goals, to increase the communication between the father and son.

The worker had involved the mother about the goal, pointing out that she would have to give the two males the opportunity to communicate during family sessions, and that would require that she talk very little.

As the worker showed the tape to me, we could clearly see the mother clenching her teeth very tightly, with her skin expanding around the jaw bone with every clench of her teeth. When the mother did talk, she discounted most progress being made by saying, "Steve still has a long way to go." This comment was typical of the mother in that she constantly discounted any progress shown by the father and the son and brought up many of their past behaviors that were "terrible."

The worker asked if he should confront the mother regarding her negative comments and about the jaw clenching. He saw the jaw clenching as her dissatisfaction with what was going on. I suggested that, instead of confronting her, he should reinforce her obvious efforts to remain quiet, as seen by her clenching her teeth to avoid speaking. At the next session, the worker praised her dedication to the contract and commented about how difficult it must be to remain quiet.

The mother said it was the only way the father would talk to his son as the father took forever to think of what he wanted to say. When the mother spoke in the session, it was to praise her son or her husband for the much better communication that was occurring between them. In future sessions, she praised the changes she saw in both the father and the son and gave the worker much credit for these changes.

This case is an example of doing the opposite of "what comes naturally" by joining the resistance rather than attacking it. When the worker was reminded of his own goal of respecting each client's efforts, he could genuinely reinforce the mother.

Instead of looking at the jaw clenching as resistance, this behavior was seen as the mother displaying her other side, her cooperative side, the side that was motivated to change.

CASE STUDY 10:
A CASE CONFERENCE WITH A
GROUP OF STUDENTS

A student was stuck in a dilemma with her supervisor about one of her clients. The student and her client both felt that significant progress had been made toward the client's primary goals. The client began to miss appointments, usually with a good excuse. Then she missed an appointment without even calling in with an excuse, although she would have to pay for the session.

The student, Marilyn, reported that her supervisor insisted that she confront the client about her avoidance behaviors, and indicate to the client that this meant that she was fearful about uncovering some significant problems within herself.

The group in the case conference felt that the missed sessions showed growth by the client, indicating that she did not presently need help. Marilyn was encouraged to express this to the client and consider stopping therapy with the client at this time.

Marilyn liked the suggestions of the group, but could not figure out how to deal with her supervisor. Because the supervisor was now the problem, the group looked for Marilyn's strengths or resources. She was asked about her own growth as a therapist and her goals for doing therapy. She quickly identified her primary goal as "being competent as a therapist." When she was asked how close she felt she was to this goal (on a scale of 1 to 10, with 10 being "competent"), she said 8 or 9. When asked what had helped her move so far toward her goal, she gave most of the credit to her supervisor.

The discussion then led to how she could tell her supervisor that she had done so much for her. Marilyn said that she could credit her growth in decision making to the supervisor and indicate that she, the student, would like to begin making decisions about clients on her own.

At the next case conference in which group members reported back on the outcomes of their action plans, Marilyn reported that the supervisor responded to the praise by saying, "I don't need to see you every week because you are now able to make decisions without supervisory input."

CASE STUDY 11:
PARENT-TEACHER CONFERENCES

A version of GFI has been used by several school systems as a way to conduct parent-teacher interviews. The teacher is placed in the role of the helper, and the purpose of the first interview in the school year (conducted in October) is to identify the goal(s) the parent has for the child. Of course, such an approach is very different from the traditional "reporting to parent" conference, in which the parent is in a one-down position of receiving information that may be critical of their child and, indirectly, of their parenting behavior.

In a demonstration of this type of interview, a mother of five children was talking about her youngest daughter who was not learning to read even though she was in the third grade. (*Reading* is a very difficult word to translate into specific performances and it is essential that it be placed in a specific setting.) As an example of nonreading behavior, the mother said that Denise, her daughter, did not even read the cereal boxes at breakfast time.

"All my kids read the cereal boxes, but Denise doesn't even do that," the mother stated emphatically. The following discussion ensued:

Teacher: What's one thing you could do that you think would make a difference in Denise's reading behavior at home?

Mother: Well, everyone in my family likes to eat. I have a rule that if you want to make something in the kitchen, you have to read the recipe first.

Teacher: And does Denise do that?

Mother: Well, not really. She makes hot chocolate, but you can do that only so many times.

Teacher: So how could you use your rule in a way that would encourage Denise to read?

Mother: I can get the recipes for her reading level and I'd have to make sure the other kids don't read them for her.

Teacher: Oh, they help her out?

Mother: All the time. They look up things for her when she's doing homework, and stuff like that.

Teacher: So they'll have to stop helping her.

Mother: That's right! And me, too.

Teacher: So connecting reading with something she likes, and making sure no one is helping her out by reading for her, are two things that might make a difference.

Mother: Right! I'm sure that would work. We've actually been part of the problem when we've done her reading for her.

Teacher: Fine. Now I'd like you to help me think of ways to carry out that type of plan in school. When I set up ways for Denise to want to read, I want you to know what I'm doing.

When a parent-teacher conference takes this form, the session moves from being a power struggle (i.e., who's at fault?) to a collaborative experience for all participants.

Past experience has shown that parents of children who are doing well readily come to their scheduled conference, whereas parents who have had an experience in which they sat through a recital of their child's deficits usually chose to avoid such negative experiences. Yet it is the parents of children who are doing poorly who teachers say are in most need of attending conferences.

SUMMARY

Using the goal-focused approach allows the parent and teacher to work together in helping the child achieve some learning goals that all parties desire. With this approach, the parent is the helpseeker in the part of the interview focused on changes at home, whereas the teacher seeks help from the parent in designing a motivational experience for the child in school. The parent is seen as someone who knows the child best. As a result, something may become different at home and at school, a difference that may lead to things being better in each environment. Of greatest importance is that this approach offers each person in the interview the opportunity to feel respected while in the presence of the other person.

9

WHEN A CLIENT AND A HELPER CANNOT TRANSFORM A PROBLEM INTO A GOAL STATEMENT

There are many client situations in which the goal is really to reduce the influence of the problem on the client's life. Some of these situations include problems like anorexia, asthma, overeating, smoking, drinking, and many other relatively compulsive behaviors.

As we look at these problems, and talk to clients about their goals, most clients will say something like, "I want to reduce my drinking, or stop it." This type of statement is considered a "dead man" goal in that the client can accomplish his goal by simply "dropping dead."

Stopping or reducing something does not fit into a well-formed goal statement because there is no active verb. In these situations, it is useful to use something similar to the White and Epston (1990) approach of "externalizing the problem." These authors emphasize that the client is not the problem—the client has a problem that influences his or her functioning. After the problem has been externalized, resources can be identified that may reduce the problem's influence. Another way of viewing this is to think about restraining the problem, just as we might restrain an aggressive child rather than attempting to aggressively control the child.

The first step in helping a client system find ways to restrain a problem is to ask clients to list the major pressures that seem to be negatively influencing the quality of their lives.

CASE STUDY 12

For example, two parents were having trouble dealing with a seventeen-year-old daughter who "wouldn't do anything her mother asked her to do." When the worker asked each family member to list the most important frustration each was experiencing, the dialogue described below occurred.

Mother: I'm afraid to ask Debbie to do anything, 'cause we end up fighting.

Father: I think Jane (the mother) is too hard on Debbie. She never backs off when there's a fight starting. I just get out of the room.

Debbie: I just can't seem to please my parents. I feel like they use me to dump some of their frustrations on.

(1) Worker: Okay, let's see if there is something in common here. Each of you has listed something about behaving ineffectively, although dad's comments were on mom's ineffectiveness.

Jane: Well, he's right. If I were an effective parent, we wouldn't be having these problems.

(2) Worker: You mean you wouldn't be fighting as much?

Jane: Right. Yes, it's like living in an armed camp, with lots of tension.

(3) Worker: Do you experience this tension at home, Debbie?

Debbie: Yes, I'm walking on eggs. Even when I do nothing I get into trouble.

(4) Worker: Would you all say that reducing the tension is your main goal?

Debbie: Yeah!

(5) Worker: What about you, Richard?

Richard: Well, Debbie seems to be looking for things to argue about. Even when we may need to discipline her brothers, she jumps into it and causes more tension.

(6) Worker: Some people might say that she was trying to take the heat off her brothers; that what she was doing was a loving act. Mom, you're shaking your head.

Mom: No. I don't agree that there is anything loving about it.

Note: Despite this poor worker move (6), the problem has been mapped out by all three family members. The worker now moves to finding positive strengths in each family member as seen by other members in order to begin to change the perspective that members have regarding each other.

(7) Worker: Good, I'm glad you're standing up for yourself and your opinions. Tell me, Jane, what are some things you're most proud of about Debbie?

Jane: Oh, lots. She's a good student, she isn't into drugs, and she's handling her dating very well. She's always been very independent, even in her thinking. It's just that . . .

(8) **Worker:** (Interrupting) Debbie, what is it like to hear your mother say those things about you?

Debbie: I'm surprised to hear them. I didn't even know she's aware of who I date. I thought she was just glad to have me out of the house.

(9) **Worker:** So now you're aware that she notices the things you do well. How does that influence the relationship between the two of you?

Debbie: I don't know.

(10) **Worker:** Does knowing she notices positive things reduce the tension between you?

Debbie: A little. But I still think she'll continue to get on me for something or other.

(11) **Worker:** Well, let's reverse what I did with your mom. What impresses you about your mom as a person?

Debbie: Oh, she's always busy, cleaning, cooking, and taking care of things around the house. And she works real hard all day and comes home tired.

(12) **Worker:** Fine! And what else?

Debbie: Well, she tries really hard to keep the peace. She is always trying to get my dad and I to understand each other. She even runs back and forth after a fight trying to clear up our misunderstandings.

(13) **Worker:** So when tension is high, she goes into shuttle diplomacy, like running back and forth from one country to another.

Jane: I sure do, and it doesn't work very well.

(14) **Worker:** Are you surprised about anything your daughter said about you, Jane?

Jane: I certainly am. I really feel unappreciated by everyone in the family.

(15) **Worker:** So you didn't know that Debbie appreciated all these things about you?

Jane: Right. I sometimes think I need a vacation, but I know that being a parent means being in charge of lots of stuff all the time.

(16) **Worker:** It strikes me that everyone is trying hard to be appreciated, so maybe feeling unappreciated is the major problem. (All three family members nod their heads.) Tell all of us, Jane, what you appreciate about yourself.

Jane: Well, I'm not sure. I feel like a failure as a mother.

(17) **Worker:** How are you with your two sons?

Jane: Fine. I have a good relationship with both of them, and very little fighting.

(18) Worker: So what's different with Debbie?

Jane: I guess 'cause she's older I expect more of her. I think she'd do more for me if she appreciated me.

(19) Worker: You mean there are ways you need her help?

Jane: Really! I'm running my head off and she doesn't see how much I need her help.

(20) Worker: Is it surprising to you, Debbie, that your mother talks about needing you?

Debbie: (Tearfully) Well, yeah! I usually feel like she only needs me to get rid of her frustrations.

(21) Worker: And now that you know she needs you as help to her, what are your thoughts?

Debbie: Beats me!

(22) Worker: Jane, would you please tell Debbie one thing you'd like help with.

Jane: Only one! Well, it would be a start if I could count on someone cooking one meal a week.

(23) Worker: So you'd appreciate coming home and not cooking once a week. You're doing a good job of asking for help. Because receiving help will likely reduce family tension, what can you ask your husband for?

Jane: Gee, that's a tough one.

(24) Worker: Well, we talked about you getting a vacation earlier.

Jane: It would be a vacation for me if I could go out for dinner after work with some coworkers and come home at nine or ten at night.

(25) Worker: Please ask Richard for that vacation.

Jane: I don't know; I feel so responsible for the family.

(26) Worker: And it seems like that feeling has led to your being unappreciated, no matter how much you did. Sort of taken for granted.

Jane: I agree, but how can I get out of it?

(27) Worker: You'll have to ask Richard that.

Jane: (Turning to Richard) How can I get out of this tension between Debbie and me?

Richard: By giving a direction to Debbie and then backing off to give it time to happen.

Jane: And if it isn't done right away?

Richard: Then there will be consequences.

Jane: So I have to change the way I'm talking to the kids. I guess . . .

(28) Worker: Wait a minute, Jane. Will you feel appreciated when you're doing what Richard is suggesting?

Jane: No! That's not what I want. That would still leave me with all the responsibility. (Turning to worker) Did I ask him in the wrong way?

(29) Worker: You're even taking responsibility now for the way you talked to Richard. And he managed to keep you as the responsible parent.

Jane: Right! (Turning to Richard) So what I want is to turn some responsibilities over to you, Richard. Like being responsible for one evening a week.

Richard: I could do that, if you didn't check on everything I did when you get home.

(30) Worker: So Richard is talking about doing something and having it appreciated. Tell me, Jane, what things do you appreciate about Richard as a contributing family member?

Jane: Well, he's certainly provided a good income for us. He's self-employed, so he has to take responsibility for everything he does.

(31) Worker: That's interesting. You mentioned earlier that Debbie was independent and now you're talking about Richard being independent. And it seems like you're declaring your independence at least one night a week.

Jane: I never thought a mother got any independence.

(32) Worker: Do you think it's possible now, with what you've heard in this session?

Jane: Well, I want to hear that I'm going to be supported for working less at home.

Richard: If you can back off and let us do some of your work, I think it'll be okay.

Debbie: I like the idea that I'll be needed for something useful instead of just taking flack.

Jane: I like thinking of independence and using it for everyone, including me. And it sure fits what you'll need to be like, Debbie, when you're at college next year.

Debbie: Speaking of college, I'll need some new clothes before I go.

Jane: Well, if you can give up a little independence and let me shop with you, I'll give up a night out with my coworkers and Richard can take care of things at home.

(33) Worker: Is that something everyone can agree on? (Richard, Debbie, and Jane all nod their heads and say "yeah" or "yes.")

Let's look back at this segment of the interview with the Stanley family. There are many problem words continually introduced throughout the transcript—fighting, tension, Debbie's independent behavior, lack of appreciation, feeling incompetent, and being exhausted (mom).

The worker obtains some general agreement to focus on tension as a problem by the time Richard answers the worker's fifth move. In addition, the worker led the client system to view independence as a resource rather than as a problem.

Other resources were found by eliciting the positive attributes the mother saw in Debbie and those Debbie saw in her mother. Asking clients to share this kind of "new" information may lead to changes in their relationship with each other, thus changing their interaction from stressful to pleasurable. This will likely reduce tension for everyone as family members show appreciation for each other.

Now I'd like you to go back through the script and identify four effective moves the worker made. Remember, an effective move is one that leads to movement by a client toward his or her goal. In this case, the goal was to *reduce the tension* at home. Tension was externalized as a problem that was influencing all relationships, and therefore something each family member had to fight against. An effective worker move would elicit a force that would help reduce the tension.

Move 1: _____

_____

_____

Move 2: _____

_____

_____

Move 3: _____

_____

_____

Move 4: _____

_____

_____

Now check the effective moves you picked with the ones identified below.

Answers:

1. (7) Good. I'm glad you're standing up for yourself and your opinions. Tell all of us, Jane, what are some things that you're most proud of about Debbie?

2. (8) Debbie, what is it like to hear your mother say these things about you?

Other effective moves were: 11, 20, 27, 29, 30, 31, 32.

This case shows clearly how, even in a family, a problem such as tension can be labeled and externalized so that clients can find resources to fight against it. Now you can go through the next case as a worker who is trying to use this approach (externalizing the problem) with an individual client.

After you have chosen one of the menu items that is closest to what you wrote in the space provided, you can look at the end of the case for a rationale for each menu item. You may want to go through the whole case first, and then compare your choices with the rationales given for each choice.

Please cover up the script following the answers at each of the 12 interactive opportunities so that you can't read what the worker actually did.

CASE STUDY 13

John is a 31-year-old white male who has been separated from his wife for about a month. There are no children. John and his wife have been through about a year of counseling and now John has been referred to you because he asked to start with a new counselor who had not seen both him and his wife.

Worker: Please pick out one stress in your life that, if you reduced it, would make your life better.

John: One stress, huh? Well, I am feeling very lonely right now.

Worker: So, the major problem that you want help with is this sense of loneliness.

John: Yes, exactly. I'm separated from my wife and we'll probably get a divorce. I don't see much hope for getting back together and I dread the loneliness I experienced before she came into my life.

You: (1) _____

_____

_____

Answers for (1):

A. ___ How long have you been together?

B. ___ You said you don't see much hope.

C. ___ How did you feel when you were lonely, before she was in your life?

D. ___ How did loneliness influence you individually, before you and your wife were together?

THE INTERVIEW CONTINUES

Worker: How did loneliness influence you individually, before you and your wife were together?

John: Oh, I'd do anything to not be alone. I'd go to Clancy's (a local bar), or call a friend, or go over to my folks'—anything but sit in my room alone.

Worker: So other people were aware of what loneliness was doing to you?

John: Maybe a few close friends. The others just accepted me when I crashed in on them, or were nice to me, like the staff at Clancy's.

Worker: So what do you think loneliness is trying to do to you?

John: Beat up on me. Get me down, so I get depressed.

Worker: And then what happens?

John: I sit in a room and play my guitar and feel sorry for myself.

Worker: So loneliness kind of takes over your life.

John: A good part of it.

Worker: And when have you won out over loneliness?

John: Well, when I got married.

Worker: So your wife helped you defeat loneliness.

John: Yeah! That's why I'm so scared now.

You: (2) _____

_____

_____

Answers for (2):

A. ___ I can understand that.

B. ___ What's scaring you?

C. ___ When you think about the time before you and your wife met and you think about who you are now, tell me how you are different.

D. ___ How are you scared now that's different from when you were scared before you were married?

THE INTERVIEW CONTINUES

Worker: When you think about the time before you met your wife and you think about who you are now, tell me how you are different.

John: Well, I'm not sure.

Worker: What small changes have occurred in you?

John: Oh, small ones. Yeah! I've grown up a lot over the past 3 years.

You: (3) _____

_____

_____

Answers for (3):

    A. ___ What has helped you grow up?

    B. ___ Why do you think that is?

    C. ___ In what ways have you noticed that?

    D. ___ On a scale from one to 10, with one being low, where were you 3 years ago and where are you now?

THE INTERVIEW CONTINUES

Worker: In what ways have you noticed that?

John: I'm not as selfish as I used to be.

Worker: Okay! What else?

John: I used to be pretty arrogant. Kind of a smart ass.

Worker: And now?

John: I don't have to act arrogant to cover my low self-esteem. I'm more accepting of my weaknesses, and I'm stronger in some ways.

Worker: What ways are those?

John: I'm a better teacher. And I'm a better son to my parents. They have both mentioned how much more mature I've been acting toward them.

You: (4) _____

_____

_____

Answers for (4):

    A. ___ What does this tell you about your own belief in yourself?

    B. ___ How can this maturity your parents have seen help you get through what's going on now?

   C. ___ How has acting more mature toward your parents changed your relationship with them?

   D. ___ Oh, so other people are noticing this growth you're aware of. Who else has noticed?

THE INTERVIEW CONTINUES

Worker: Oh, so other people are noticing this growth you're aware of. Who else has noticed?

John: Oh, my principal at school. And a couple of teachers have said some nice things that they heard from parents or kids. And a few close friends have mentioned that I have more depth.

Worker: What ways could this new depth help you defeat the loneliness you're expecting back in your life?

John: Well, definitely my friends. They've already rallied around me, either by coming to my house or by inviting me to crash with them.

Worker: So you've already started to fend off loneliness. Does anyone or anything from work influence your keeping loneliness away?

John: Yeah! My principal recommended me for some training in teaching math. The superintendent gave me $1,000 to go to California for this training. It starts next week and lasts 3 weeks.

You: (5) _____

_____

_____

Answers for (5):

   A. ___ How do you account for actively seeking this training opportunity and the financial support to help you?

   B. ___ Was your wife going to go with you to California?

   C. ___ Did you apply for this opportunity before you separated from your wife?

   D. ___ How did you happen to seek this training opportunity?

THE INTERVIEW CONTINUES

Worker: How do you account for actively seeking this training opportunity and the financial support to help you?

John: Well, I attended a week-long session on this approach to teaching math on Cape Cod and I thought it was the best approach I'd ever heard about. I didn't get anything this good in my college classes, either undergrad or graduate.

Worker: I notice that you have the ability to tell when something will be useful to your students.

John: Yeah! I've become good at separating the baloney from the good stuff.

Worker: And you care about your students enough to want them to get the good stuff, like going to Cape Cod for that training.

John: To be honest, I spent a lot of summers in Cape Cod with my folks, and it was a good excuse to go back there.

You: (6) _____

_____

_____

Answers for (6):

A. ___ You gave yourself a good whack just then by putting yourself down for something rather than taking credit for deciding to go to the training, and seeking financial support, and doing these things to help the kids in your class.

B. ___ What else led you to seek that learning opportunity?

C. ___ What do you like about Cape Cod?

D. ___ Well, I can understand that. I've been to Cape Cod and I loved it.

THE INTERVIEW CONTINUES

Worker: You gave yourself a good whack just then by putting yourself down for something, rather than taking credit for deciding to go to the training, and seeking financial support, and doing these things to help the kids in your class.

John: Yeah! I do that a lot to myself. (Chuckle) I call it downing myself, and I'm even doing it here.

Worker: And what could you say about yourself and this training that would stop you from downing yourself?

John: Well, I could say that the reason I'm going to the training is that I'd heard a lot of word-of-mouth about the program, and it was all real positive, regarding how it helped kids.

Worker: Word of mouth about what, specifically?

John: That kids really learned to understand math with this approach.

Worker: So being an effective teacher has been an important goal for you?

John: Yes, I really love teaching and watching the kids I have each year grow as the year goes on.

Worker: And this love for teaching has grown continuously with you?

John: Absolutely. I'm quite confident about myself as a teacher, and I want to get better at influencing the learning opportunities for my kids.

You: (7) _____

_____

_____

Answers for (7):

A. ___ Who or what has helped you to achieve this growing confidence in yourself?

B. ___ In what way are you better now than you were a few years ago?

C. ___ Why have your students improved over the last few years?

D. ___ As your confidence has grown as a teacher, how has your relationship with students changed?

THE INTERVIEW CONTINUES

Worker: Who or what has helped you to achieve this growing confidence in yourself?

John: Well, other people. And inside me, a part of me tells me to focus on helping kids learn and to ignore all the political garbage that goes on in school.

Worker: I'm impressed with how well you can ignore negatives and move on toward your goals at school. How might you draw from that part of you to help you deal with loneliness?

John: I haven't thought about doing that before.

You: (8) _____

_____

_____

Answers for (8):

A. ___ Think about it now.

B. ___ How are you weaker as a result of your fear of loneliness?

C. ___ Then maybe it's not a good idea.

D. ___ Why not?

THE INTERVIEW CONTINUES

Worker: Think about it now.

John: I know a little bit about thought control and focusing on positive thinking.

Worker: So that's a resource you can draw on. What else will help you fight against loneliness?

John: The inner confidence that I'll get through this somehow.

Worker: Where does that confidence come from?

John: I don't know. It's just there.

You: (9) _____

_____

_____

Answers for (9):

A. ____ Why is it there?

B. ____ How do you use it to help you get through these times?

C. ____ How do you know it's there?

D. ____ What do you notice that tells you that you have this confidence?

THE INTERVIEW CONTINUES

Worker: How do you know it's there?

John: There's this inner calmness, a really relaxed feeling in my stomach.

Worker: And you use that relaxed feeling to deal with what?

John: Some of the panic I experience when things aren't going too well.

Worker: Would you say this relaxed feeling will help you deal with loneliness?

John: Definitely!

Worker: Picture the next month for me, when you're being this confident, relaxed person.

John: Well, when I'm alone I'll be playing my guitar and maybe singing.

Worker: In your living room?

John: Yeah, with my two cats around.

You: (10) _____

_____

_____

Answers for (10):

A. ___ And what will you be singing?

B. ___ How will this be different from the past?

C. ___ And when you're not alone, what will you be doing?

D. ___ And you'll be feeling confident about yourself and your future at that time?

THE INTERVIEW CONTINUES

Worker: And what will you be singing?

John: I don't know for sure. Whatever comes out of me. I won't purposely choose any song.

Worker: As you see yourself in that scene, what will you be experiencing internally?

John: That relaxation I was talking about.

Worker: What other things, besides playing music, will bring out that relaxed feeling?

John: Talking with people—my friends, my folks?

Worker: And what else?

John: Well, some new things and even some new people.

Worker: Uh huh! (Head nod)

John: Well, I was at a wedding last week in Maryland, and I met this great gal, and we got along really well.

You: (11) _____

_____

_____

Answers for (11):

A. ___ So you've already started to develop new relationships, to move onto this new path in your life.

B. ___ Does it surprise you that you were able to get along so well with her?

C. ___ What does getting along well with her tell you about your future?

D. ___ Have you ever "clicked" that quickly with someone right after you met them?

THE INTERVIEW CONTINUES

Worker: What does getting along with her so well tell you about your future?

John: That maybe someone new will be a part of my life. It's exciting to be thinking about meeting different women. It's so unpredictable.

Worker: Your face shows you're excited about some unpredictable things in the future.

John: Yeah. I'm feeling kind of amazed that I'm looking forward to an unpredictable future.

Worker: You could always give up on people and spend your time alone, being predictably miserable.

John: That's a fact! (Laughter) That's what I've been doing.

Worker: And so it amazes you to plan on being different?

John: Well, planning to meet new people was one of my greatest fears in the past.

You: (12) _____

_____

_____

Answers for (12):

    A. ___ So you have these new beliefs about yourself, as relaxed, more confident, and moving into new relationships.

    B. ___ Do you think you'll continue to be amazed about these new ideas you have about your future?

    C. ___ Do you think the scary feelings will stop you from seeking new relationships?

    D. ___ What do you see holding you back?

THE INTERVIEW CONCLUDES

Worker: So you have these new beliefs about yourself, as relaxed, more confident, and moving into new relationships.

John: Well, yes, regarding the training in California and a trip up north where I'll be with some new people, just like in California.

Worker: So these two trips will involve new experiences for you. They will give you a good chance to keep on with these new beliefs you have about yourself.

John: Oh yeah! I'll meet lots of new people at the training, and I think it will open up lots of possibilities for my future career. I think I'm gaining some confidence in my ability to deal with whatever life hands me.

Worker: You look very confident right now. I think that's a good note to end our session on. I'll look over my notes and write you a letter reflecting on our session together.

John: I'd like that. No therapist has ever done that before.

Rationales for (1)

A. This is a good example of a curiosity question, and one that will not produce any information related to dealing with the loneliness problem.

B. This move focuses on a deficit and may lead to increasing the sense of hopelessness.

C. This move seeks feelings about loneliness rather than effective ways of minimizing the influence of the loneliness.

D. This preferred move seeks to map the problem's influence on the client when he was alone as he is now. The move immediately externalizes loneliness.

Rationales for (2)

A. This move reinforces being scared and implies that the worker can put himself or herself in the client's shoes.

B. This move reinforces the client's deficit word *scared* and is redundant because it is clear that what is scaring the client is the lack of support available from his wife, a support that no longer exists.

C. This preferred move asks for the client to identify changes in himself over 3 years, thus eliciting any growth he is aware of or, possibly, any lack of growth.

D. Though seeking differences, this move focuses entirely on the problem word *scared*.

Rationales for (3)

A. This is a good move, seeking client resources related to growing up.

B. This cause-seeking question may find resources, so it is not totally inappropriate.

C. This preferred move is intended to elicit the evidence the client has experienced that tells him he's grown up. He may be surprised by what he finds out about himself as he searches for this evidence.

D. Because the client has already said he *has* grown, scaling this change is largely unnecessary.

Rationales for (4)

A. A good move intended to lead the client to focus on himself by reflecting about what other people's comments meant to him.

B. A good move asking John to use the resource he has just identified.

C. A good move designed to elicit how some changes in John's behavior may have influenced important relationships. The move also presupposes that changes have occurred, leading John to confidently look for such changes.

D. This move, slightly preferred, stays on the focus of John's growth being noticed by others, in the hope of strengthening the growth even further.

Rationales for (5)

A. This preferred move seeks to lead John to look for either internal or external resources that have helped him take positive actions.

B. This closed question seems intended to meet the worker's curiosity.

C. This closed question seems to emphasize a detective's approach to analyzing John's past behavior.

D. This is a good move, similar to (1) but not stated as specifically regarding John's positive actions.

Rationales for (6)

A. This is the preferred move, with a light confrontation regarding John's self-deprecating message, followed by a reinforcement of his positive efforts. It is also purposely stated as a closed statement, seeking John's agreement or disagreement.

B. This is a good move seeking to find more professional reasons (i.e., teaching) for seeking to go for training.

C. This is a poor move, simply seeking information that may tend to justify John's personal reasons for going to Cape Cod.

D. This move obviously focuses on the wrong aspect of the interview and puts the worker's personal viewpoint into the interaction.

Rationales for (7)

A. This preferred move seeks external or internal resources that have helped John gain confidence as a teacher.

B. A good move seeking positive differences John sees in himself as a teacher.

C. A cause-seeking move that is unlikely to lead anywhere because such improvement would have multiple causes, and the improvement would be hard to verify.

D. A good move that is an example of connecting differences in behavior to changes in relationships, with the presupposition that such changes have occurred.

Rationales for (8)

Please write your own rationales for the menu items for the last five interventions in this interview. Then compare what you wrote with those provided at the end of this chapter.

1._____
_____
_____

2._____
_____
_____

3._____
_____
_____

4._____
_____
_____

Rationales for (9)

1._____
_____
_____

2._____
_____
_____

3._____
_____
_____

4._____
_____
_____

Rationales for (10)

1._____
_____
_____

2._____
_____
_____

3._____
_____
_____

4._____
_____
_____

Rationales for (11)

1._____
_____
_____

2._____
_____
_____

3._____
_____
_____

4._____
_____
_____

Rationales for (12)

1._____
 _____
 _____

2._____
 _____
 _____

3._____
 _____
 _____

4._____
 _____
 _____

Rationales for (8)

1. A preferred move using John's language and focusing on this moment in the interview.
2. A deficit-focused question that will likely elicit negative statements by John about himself.
3. A fair statement in that it allows John to decide whether to try to use this "new" part.
4. A cause-seeking question that tends to lead John into the past to find reasons for *not* doing something. This could produce guilt in John.

Rationales For (9)

1. This *why* question is very similar to the previous question that John has answered with "I don't know."
2. A good move, seeking how John uses an identified resource.
3. The preferred move, eliciting the evidence John can find that verifies for himself that he has confidence.
4. Similar to (3) above, and very good.

Rationales for (10)

1. A leading question simply seeking to anchor John more completely in his image of his desirable state.

2. A fair question, but it leads John out of experiencing the desired state more completely.

3. A move that simply doesn't fit this moment in the interview.

4. A move that involves the worker reading John's feelings *for* him, rather than eliciting these feelings from him.

Rationales for (11)

1. A closed statement seeking John's agreement or disagreement about moving positively into the future. Such a move is intended to seek a commitment before moving forward and is a good move.

2. A closed question intended to lead John to reflect on the impact of his new relationship on his view of himself. This reflection may strengthen John's self-image.

3. A preferred move that reinforces a strength and leads John to think about how that strength can influence his future.

4. A closed question that seems totally unnecessary because either a *yes* or a *no* can be difficult to build on regarding strengthening John's confidence in himself.

Rationales for (12)

1. A preferred closed statement, seeking to reinforce the strengths already identified and connect them to the future.

2. A good closed question building off John's word *amazed* and seeking to connect it to the future.

3. A deficit-focused question emphasizing a negative word John hasn't used for quite awhile, thus possibly leading him back to his problem state.

4. A poor move emphasizing obstacles at a time in the interview when John is focusing on strengths.

SUMMARY

The two cases in this chapter demonstrate instances when the goal of therapy is to find resources that diminish the impact of the problem on the client's life. These resources are most often found by leading the help-seeker(s) to another side or part of themselves. As they explore their own uniqueness, either internally or by finding unique ways they have acted in the past, the worker/client unit discovers many potential resources that can change the client's situation. Such an approach is essential in dealing with problems that will never be "cured" or totally overcome.

10

A FEW CLOSING THOUGHTS

Throughout this book, I have written about three kinds of thinking—critical, constructive, and creative. I have emphasized that the helper-client system should carry out the latter two kinds of thinking in order to increase the possible ways a client system might find to achieve change. For a very fresh look at thinking processes, I recommend that readers turn to the works of Dr. Edward de Bono (1990), with particular reference to the book, *I Am Right, You Are Wrong.*

The material below draws together some of his ideas, with changes designed to fit a helper-client situation.

OUR TASK

Design experiences for clients that unleash their constructive and creative thinking, rather than their critical thinking.

ANALYSIS

We are good at analysis. You may be uncomfortable and analysis determines that you are sitting on a pin. Remove the pin and all is well. Yet most problems don't lend themselves to finding one cause that can be eliminated.

FURTHERMORE

For most problems, we cannot be certain of any cause; or if we can find some causes, we cannot remove them—for example, human greed; or there may be a multiplicity of causes. Traditionally, we continue to analyze problems further and analyze the analysis of others (research). Has any research study regarding human beings ever ended without saying that further research is needed?

WORSHIPPING HISTORY

Our over-analysis of client deficits may be driven by an obsession—in the larger world and in therapy—with history. This view sees helping a client as leading them to learn more about their history without considering that many historians have said that there may be no such thing as history. There are only stories told by people, each with his or her own perspective regarding what happened. Stories about problems tend to increase the severity of each problem, or tend to find more problems.

AN ALTERNATIVE TO ANALYSIS

What is needed is to design a way out of the problem. This can be done by identifying the desired state (goal) and finding ways to move toward that goal.

A FUTURE FOCUS

When we focus on designing the future, we allow all parties to partake in both creative and constructive types of thinking.

WHAT IS DESIGNING

We are designing when we look for the consequences of actions; when we consider what forces are supporting change, and what forces are pulling toward the status quo; when we rank our priorities; when we define goals or objectives. Designing means doing more idea work and less information work. Designing means emphasizing the skills of doing more than the skills of knowing; through emphasizing both the helper's and the client's competencies.

A LAST WORD ON HISTORY

Plants thrive in dirt but people don't do well when planted in their own dirt.

APPENDIX A

INTRODUCTION

The two appendixes that follow are designed to give the reader very explicit practice in using the major concepts presented in the text of this book.

Appendix A includes a section of programmed material designed to test the reader's understanding of four vital skills for a goal-focused interviewer to master.

1. Recognizing partial goal statements.
2. Recognizing and eliciting client resources.
3. Recognizing and limiting problem information so that problem talking is minimized.
4. Helping clients design change plans.

Appendix B includes a series of exercises for teachers to use when training a group of people to be goal-focused interviewers. The exercises are written in explicit detail so that they can be used by any group of people who wish to practice what was learned through reading this book.

FORMS IN GOAL-FOCUSED INTERVIEWING

This program offers you a methodical way of learning how to identify typical verbal forms clients use in helping interviews.

You will be directed to read selected scripts from many sources, including literature. Scripts will be analyzed for specific forms or segments common to goal-setting interviews. Avoid arguing with the form analysis until you understand how the theory views the evidence cited. Then, of course, you may decide to accept or reject all or parts of the theory.

Having completed the unit, you should be able to

1. Identify four forms found in goal-setting interviews.
2. Identify invasion of one form with another.

FRAME #1

This program will apply the analysis of forms to the study of scripts of human interaction. The purpose in this application is to help you recognize the forms quickly so that you can place most client communications into a goal-focused context.

There are four basic forms found in most helping interviews:

Goal Statements
Resources
Problem Information
Action Plans

RECOGNIZING GOAL STATEMENTS

Each form has basic criteria that must be met. These criteria are called stresses. There are two basic stresses for goal statements:

1. Goal statements picture new or increased actions in specific settings.
2. Goal statements include specific descriptions of the desired outcomes the actions are intended to achieve.

For example, a client (a housewife with three small children) said: "I need to get away from my children during the day."

This statement was clarified several times, so that it was more specific, as shown when the client said: "If I could spend only one hour three times a week outside the house with someone over 21 and discuss current events, I'd be able to take my home life."

The two stresses contained in the goal statement are a) New actions in a specific setting three times a week, and b) [the desired outcome] "being able to take my home life."

Now, please read the statements below, then place an "X" in front of any statement that seems *less* likely to be a description of a client goal.

1.___ The group listening to Janet wished to know where her father was.
2.___ I wish my dad would fix up a place I can have to myself so that I can study with no interruptions.

3.___ I'm starting to bring my grades up now. My father has been talking to the teachers to find out what's bothering me so I can bring them up. So far I got the A in History he wanted, and in Algebra I've handed in all my homework.

4.___ Yeah, my mom and dad want me to go see a brain surgeon. 'Cause, see, I get dizzy and then I pass out. And I get up in the middle of the night and pace the floor. Once I got up about 12:00 and cleaned the house until 6:00. Then I went back to bed and got up 12 hours later.

ANSWER TO FRAME #1

An X is placed in front of the statements that are *less* likely to meet the requirements for a well-formed goal statement.

1. _x_ The group listening to Janet wished to know where her father was.
2. _x_ I wish my dad would fix up a place I can have to myself so that I can study with no interruptions.
3. _x_ I'm starting to bring my grades up now. My father has been talking to the teachers to find out what's bothering me, so I can bring them up. So far I got the A in History he wanted, and in Algebra I've handed in all my homework.

(When a client talks about someone else, he or she is not talking about his or her goals. This material "invades" the form by focusing on her father's goals. We will be discussing form invasion later.)

4. _x_ Yeah, my mom and dad want me to go see a brain surgeon. 'Cause, see, I get dizzy and then I pass out. And, I get up in the middle of the night and pace the floor. Once I got up about 12:00 and cleaned the house until 6:00. Then I went back to bed and got up twelve hours later.

The main principle identified in these statements is that goal statements must refer to something the client wants, not something someone else wants for her.

FRAME #2
RECOGNIZING AND ELICITING CLIENT RESOURCES

Resources include means to an end; that is, something that will help a client achieve one goal. Resources are usually stated as one word, or a brief phrase, without an emphasis on specifics.

In the script below, the problem the client initially stated is her relatively constant headaches at work. Please read the script provided and then answer the questions that follow the script.

Therapist: When was the last time you had a headache?
Client: Yesterday. I had one yesterday. It wasn't too bad. It was on the right side and ran down my neck and I took two aspirins about 3 in the afternoon. They didn't help much.

Therapist: Do you usually take aspirin?

Client: No, I take Darvon, but I was out of it that day.

Therapist: You said you took them at 3 o'clock. Is that when you got the headache?

Client: No. I had the headache about 10:30 or 11 o'clock. It wasn't too bad then.

Therapist: Did you have it when you got to school? (Note: client teaches in a junior high school).

Client: No. I remember feeling okay when I went to the homeroom and, ah, and the, ah . . . (Sigh) . . . I've got these students. The principal says it's because I'm the only one that is a good disciplinarian in the school. He gives me all these problem children to teach and, uh, but they don't . . . I run a tight ship and they don't make noise, but I have to be firm with them. I have to be stern.

Therapist: And what troubles you about that?

Client: Well, I—I don't see why I should get all these problems. I don't enjoy this.

Therapist: It sounds like there are a good many things that are bothering you in addition to headaches.

Client: Yes . . . Well, the school. I shouldn't be in the school I'm in but I haven't done anything about it. I'm teaching seventh grade, and I should . . . I'd like to go to the high school. I want to enjoy teaching like I used to. I enjoyed students when they were interested in learning.

Obviously, if we are to correctly identify resources that will help achieve one client goal, we must first identify some general client goal statements. Please write one or two goals in the space below that you read in the script.

Goal Statements:

1. _____
2. _____

Now, write two resources that would help the client move toward each goal you identified.

Goal 1   1. _____.
         2. _____.
Goal 2   1. _____.
         2. _____.

ANSWERS FOR FRAME #2

Goal Statements (General, not well formed)

1. More days with no headaches at school.
2. Movement to a school where she enjoys teaching without being stern and students will exhibit learning behaviors.

Resources include

Goal 1   1. Take aspirin
         2. Take Darvon
Goal 2   1. She is aware that she hasn't taken the actions necessary to move to the high school.
         2. She had a positive teaching experience when her students were learning.

These resources would be reinforced after the client stated them. Then the worker and the client will choose one goal (at this time). The helper will then lead the client to develop a well-formed goal statement and verify that the resources already identified will be useful in achieving the goal. Additional resources can also be identified so that the client believes that he or she has the resources necessary to achieve the goal.

FRAME #3
PROBLEM FORMS

You have probably been surprised to be exposed to material on goals and resources without receiving any training on identifying problem forms. This sequence has been purposeful because there is considerable evidence to show that collecting problem information first can be dysfunctional to helping clients develop plans for achieving their goals.

The position taken in this material is that problem information is elicited only after a goal has been selected and only when it describes an obstacle to using a resource. Please note that the helper doesn't prevent a client from problem talking. Rather, the helper avoids using behaviors that encourage problem talking, while using behaviors that promote goal identification.

To place this concept in perspective, the chart below may be useful:

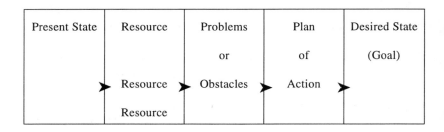

Present State	Resource	Problems or Obstacles	Plan of Action	Desired State (Goal)
	Resource			
	Resource			

The two stresses for identifying problem forms are cited below:

1. Problem forms refer to a specific existing situation, both a condition and a setting in which the condition exists for the client.
2. Problem forms refer to the client's internal or external (interactional) difficulties. Descriptions of other people are not considered to be in problem form.

Please check any statements below that could be classified as problem information:

1.___ Well, my husband doesn't understand me.
2.___ My main worry about Mark (my son) is that he doesn't know how to succeed at school.
3.___ The mother stated, "If a teacher doesn't have any respect for a student, why should the student have any respect for a teacher?"
4.___ My dad comes home drunk all the time. He breaks everything in the house. He broke my mother's dishwasher.
5.___ Yesterday I got a phone call and my father answered and he was really drunk. So he says, "No, she isn't in right now." He did that twice and he wouldn't tell me who it was.

ANSWERS FOR FRAME #3

1.___ Well, my husband doesn't understand me. (This statement is very general, with no setting specified.)
2._x_ My main worry about Mark (my son) is that he doesn't know how to succeed at school.
3.___ The mother stated, "If a teacher doesn't have any respect for a student, why should the student have any respect for a teacher?" (This statement is a rationale that defends someone, but that's all we know.)
4.___ My dad comes home drunk all the time. He breaks everything in the house. He broke my mother's dishwasher. (This information doesn't include the client.)
5.___ Yesterday I got a phone call and my father answered and he was real drunk. So he says, "No, she isn't in right now." He did that twice and he wouldn't tell me who it was. (This information focuses on blaming someone other than the speaker).

The following is a script that you can use to practice identifying statements that are in problem form.

EXHIBIT FOR FRAME #4

Please read the script below and then answer the questions provided at the end of the script. This is a transcription of the first 5 minutes of a professional-parent interview.

Setting:

A mother has asked to talk with a school staff member about her 8-year-old son, Ralph.

P: Will you sit there? I'm Mr. Murray. You're Mrs. Green, aren't you? What brings you here?

M: Everything's wrong. Everybody here at school is ignoring my requests for help for my son. My husband won't lift a finger. It makes me irritable, tense, depressed.

P: Go on.

M: I don't feel like talking right now.

P: You don't (Pause). Do you sometimes?

M: That's the trouble, I get too wound up to talk. If I get started, I'm all right.

P: Well, perhaps you will get started.

M: Could I have a cup of coffee?

P: Sure, we made some; there are a lot of parent interviews being conducted today. (Gets cup) What do you do?

M: I'm a nurse but my husband won't let me work.

P: What do you mean, he won't let you work?

M: (Clears throat) Well, (Clears throat) for instance, I—I'm supposed to do some relief duty 2 weeks this month—next month, in December. And he always makes it so miserable for me that I'm in a constant stew. And he says that my place is in the home with the children. I agree. But I—I need a rest. I need to get away from them . . . I need to be with, well, with people. I can't stay closeted up in the house all the time.

(Pause)

P: How many kids are there?

M: Two, besides Ralph.

FRAME #4

Check which of the statements below from the exhibit fit the problem statement criteria (cited in Frame #3).

1. ___ Everything's wrong.
2. ___ Everybody here at school is ignoring my requests for help for my son.
3. ___ My husband won't lift a finger.
4. ___ It makes me irritable, tense, depressed.
5. ___ I need a rest.
6. ___ I need to be with, well, with people.

ANSWERS FOR FRAME #4

1. ___ Everything's wrong. (Very general.)
2. _x_ Everybody here at school is ignoring my requests for help for my son.

3. ___ My husband won't lift a finger. (Describing someone else.)

4. ___ It makes me irritable, tense, depressed. (Doesn't describe a setting for the problem.)

5. ___ I need a rest.

6. ___ I need to be with, well, with people.

Notes: 5. is a vague goal statement. 6. is a good beginning goal statement. However, it should be connected to her son, Ralph, as well as specifying where she would like to be with people.

An excerpt from John Steinbeck's *The Grapes of Wrath* (1939/1993) follows. After reading the page, nine brief segments will be repeated so that you can practice choosing between goal statements and problem statements.

EXHIBIT FOR FRAME #5
EXCERPT FROM *THE GRAPES OF WRATH*

Tom went on. "I'd like to say—well, that preacher he wants to come along with us." He was silent. His words lay in the group, and the group was silent. "He's a nice fella," Tom added. "We've knowed him a long time. Talks a little wild sometimes, but he talks sensible." And he relinquished the proposal to the family.

The light was going gradually. Ma left the group and went into the house, and the iron clang of the stove came from the house. In a moment she walked back to the brooding council.

Grampa said, "There's two ways a thinkin'. Some folks use'ta figger that a preacher was poison luck."

Tom said, "This fella said he ain't a preacher no more."

Grampa waved his hand back and forth. "Once a fella's a preacher, he's always a preacher. That's somepin' you can't get shut of. They was some folks figgered it was a good respectable thing to have a preacher along. If somebody died, preacher buried 'em. Weddin' come due, or overdue, an' there's your preacher. Baby come, an' you got a christener right under the roof. Me, I always said they was preachers an' preachers. Got to pick 'em. I kinda like this fella. He ain't stiff."

Pa dug his stick into the dust and rolled it between his fingers so that it bored a little hole. "They's more to this than is he lucky, or is he a nice fella," Pa said. "We got to figger close. It's a sad thing to figger close. Let's see, now, there's Grampa and Grandma—that's eight. Rosesharen an' Connie is ten, an' Ruthie an' Winfiel' is twelve. We got to take the dogs 'cause what'll we do else? Can't shoot a good dog, an' there ain't nobody to give 'em to. An' that's fourteen."

"Not countin' what chickens is left, an' two pigs," said Noah.

Pa said, 'I aim to get those pigs salted down to eat on the way. We gonna need meat. Carry the salt kegs right with us. But I'm wonderin' if we can all ride, an' the preacher too. An' kin we feed an extra mouth?" Without turning his head, he asked, "Kin we, Ma?"

Ma cleared her throat. "It ain't kin we?" she said firmly. "As far as 'kin, we can't do nothin', not go to California or nothin'; but as far as will, why, we'll do what we are willing to do. As far as 'will'—it's a long time our folks been here and east before, an' I never heard tell of no Joads or no Haxletts, neither, ever refusin' food an' shelter or a lift on the road to anybody that asked. They's been mean Joads, but never that mean."

Pa broke in, "But s'pose there just ain't room?" He had twisted his neck to look up at her, and he was ashamed. Her tone had made him ashamed. "S'pose we jus' can't all get in the truck?"

"There ain't room now," she said. "There ain't room for more'n six, an' twelve is goin' sure. One more ain't gonna hurt; an' a man, strong an' healthy, ain't never no burden. An' anytime when we got two pigs an' over a hundred dollars, an' we wonderin' if we kin feed a fella—" She stopped, and Pa turned back, and his spirit was raw from the whipping.

Grandma said, "A preacher is a nice thing to be with us. He gave us a nice grace this morning."

Pa looked at the face of each one for dissent, and then he said, "I want you to call 'im over, Tommy. If he's goin', he ought ta be here."

FRAME #5

From the Exhibit for Frame #7, identify any sentence that is a goal statement (GS) or a problem statement (PS). Leave any blank that are neither a GS nor a PS.

1. ___ But I'm wonderin' if we can all ride, an' the preacher too.
2. ___ Some folks use 'ta figger that a preacher was poison luck.
3. ___ Once a fella's a preacher, he's always a preacher.
4. ___ Can't shoot a good dog, an' there ain't nobody to give 'em to.
5. ___ I want you to call 'em over, Tommy. If he's goin', he ought ta be here.
6. ___ The preacher, he wants to come along with us.
7. ___ We'll do what we are willing to do.
8. ___ There ain't room now.
9. ___ I never heard tell of no Joads or no Hazletts, neither, ever refusin' food an' shelter or a lift on the road to anybody who asked.

Now compare your answers with those provided.

ANSWERS FOR FRAME #5

1. _PS_ But I'm wondering if we can all ride, and the preacher too.
2. _PS_ Some folks use to figure that a preacher was poison luck.
3. _PS_ Once a fella's a preacher, he's always a preacher.
4. _PS_ Can't shoot a good dog, and there ain't nobody to give him to.
5. _GS_ I want you to call him over, Tommy. If he's goin', he ought to be here.

6. __GS__ The preacher, he wants to come along with us.
7. _____ We'll do what we're willing to do.
8. __PS__ There ain't room now.
9. _____ I never heard tell of no Joads or no Hazletts neither ever refusing food an' shelter or a lift on the road to anyone who asked.

Note: 7 and 9 are resources that can be used to decide whether to take the preacher along. You might have labeled them as goal statements. They are both examples of how all verbal communication does not fit perfectly in any given form.

FRAME #6
ACTION PLAN

The last form to be taught in this material is the Action Plan form. Action Plans have two basic criteria, as described below.

1. They tell: Who; Will do what; When; Where
2. They contain means for plotting progress toward the goal. (How will you know you're arriving?)

Example:

Worker: Well, Mrs. Jones, let me summarize. You seem to have decided to use a trial separation as the best approach to help decide whether you will get a divorce. Your first step is to get out of your apartment quickly with the kids and your personal belongings before your husband returns home from hunting. You'll call your sister to help you but you'll live in an apartment on the other side of town because your husband will look at your sister's place. You'll get financial help from your church and apply for AFDC immediately. You also plan to check on getting your old job back. Does that seem to cover it?

Client: Yes, except that we said I would see you here in 2 days to tell you what has happened because all of these things have to go right or I'll need other help.

Worker: Fine, 2 o'clock will be okay with me on Thursday. How about you?

As you can see, detailed action plans are easily identified. Everyday life offers countless opportunities to identify brief action plans simply by listening to or reading commercials. Almost every commercial identifies a problem and wants you to buy the product as a resource for achieving your goal. What the product is supposed to do is part of the plan of action. Who purchases it—when, and where—are all parts of the action plan. For instance, installing an automatic garage door opener is a resource for achieving goals such as securing the items in the garage.

Your actual plan of action would cover buying the automatic door opener and either installing it yourself or arranging installation by a certain date.

To clarify the difference between goal statements (GS), resources (R), and action plans (AP), please check the appropriate column for each statement below. (Note: Many statements will be partial goal statements, rather than complete ones. Please label those partial goal statements with a GS.)

GS **R** **AP**

___ ___ ___ a. I want the dry, natural look.

___ ___ ___ b. A hair spray that is dry when applied.

___ ___ ___ c. Try three different sprays and select the one your wife thinks makes you look natural.

___ ___ ___ d. I'd like to reduce Dick's fighting.

___ ___ ___ e. Meet with Dick and one of the boys he fights with.

___ ___ ___ f. Talk with five kids in Dick's class at school where fighting occurs.

___ ___ ___ g. Talk with the entire class about Dick's fighting.

___ ___ ___ h. I wish Dick would get involved in positive experiences in school.

___ ___ ___ i. Train Dick in alternative responses when he is angry.

___ ___ ___ j. Meet with Dick and his major opponent three times a week to help them learn alternative ways of responding to each other's teasing. In each session, they would see alternative responses modeled, practice using the responses, get feedback on their responses, and then try to interact again.

___ ___ ___ k. I hate my job.

___ ___ ___ l. I want to learn to interact and respond effectively to potential employers.

___ ___ ___ m. Identify attractive jobs by talking with the people who work in settings I'm interested in; then practicing employment interviews for jobs in those settings.

ANSWERS TO FRAME #6

GS	R	AP	
x	—	—	a. I want the dry, natural look.
—	x	—	b. A hair spray that is dry when applied.
—	—	x	c. Try three different sprays and select the one your wife thinks makes you look natural.
x	—	—	d. I'd like to reduce Dick's fighting.
—	x	—	e. Meet with Dick and one of the boys he fights with.
—	x	—	f. Talk with five kids in Dick's class at school where fighting occurs.
—	x	—	g. Talk with the entire class about Dick's fighting.
x	—	—	h. I wish Dick would get involved in positive experiences in school.
—	x	—	i. Train Dick in alternative responses when he is angry.
—	—	x	j. Meet with Dick and his major opponent three times a week to help them learn alternative ways of responding to each other's teasing. In each session, they would see alternative responses modeled, practice using the responses, get feedback on their responses, and then try to interact again.
—	—	—	k. I hate my job.*
x	—	—	l. I want to learn to interact and respond effectively to potential employers.
—	—	x	m. Identify attractive jobs by talking with the people who work in settings I'm interested in; then practicing employment interviews for jobs in those settings.

*This is a problem statement.

FRAME #7

As a review, please write in your own words the eight stresses or criteria for each of the four forms in goal-setting interviews.

GOAL STATEMENTS

1. _____
   _____

2. _____
   _____

RESOURCES

3. _____
   _____

4. _____
   _____

PROBLEM FORMS

5. _____
   _____

6. _____
   _____

ACTION PLANS

7. _____
   _____

8. _____
   _____

Now compare what you wrote with the following answers.

ANSWERS FOR FRAME #7

The eight stresses of goal setting are

1. Goal statements picture new or increased client behaviors in specific settings.
2. Goal statements include specific descriptions of the desired outcomes the actions are intended to achieve.

3. Resources describe means to an end, not the end itself.
4. Resources are stated in one word or a brief phrase with the specifics left to the action plan.
5. Problem statements refer to the help seeker.
6. Problem statements refer to specific settings.
7. Action plans tell: a) who; b) will do what; c) when; 4) where.
8. Action plans include specified means for plotting progress toward the goal.

APPENDIX B: TRAINING EXERCISES FOR GOAL-FOCUSED INTERVIEWING

EXERCISE 1:
HOW YOUR BELIEFS OR VALUES INFLUENCE THE WAY YOU FUNCTION AS A HELPER

This exercise is designed to offer several significant learning experiences for participants.

In small groups each participant (as an interviewee) will have the opportunity to collaborate with one person (the interviewer) in eliciting the major beliefs that guide the interviewee's work as a helper. The interviewer will direct the overall process by using strength-focused questions intended to help the interviewee find his or her internal values that provide direction to helping behaviors. In addition, the interviewer will guide the interviewee to identify goals the interviewee considers vital to ensure positive growth as a helping person.

SOME BASIC PRINCIPLES FOR CONDUCTING THIS EXERCISE

1. Self-Handicapping Generalizations

   The interviewer should listen carefully for generalizations stated by the interviewee. When a self-handicapping generalization is stated, such as "I'm just a beginner," the following questions may dislodge this habitual thinking pattern:

   a. What are some of the strengths that a beginner can offer a client?

   or

   b. What can you offer a client that an experienced helper (who may be somewhat burned out) wouldn't be able to offer a client?

2. Eliciting Resources

When the interviewee uses contractions in his or her sentences, such as "I can't," "I haven't," or "I don't," respond with questions such as:

a. What would it be like if you could do this?

or

b. If you did something that you usually don't do, tell me what you would be doing.

3. Seeking Positive Alternatives or Unique Outcomes

When the interviewee talks about something that "sticks" him or her as a helper, look for a third or a fourth way of doing what he or she wants to do.

For example, an interviewee said, "I can't think of how to help a person who complains about their life but refuses to take any of my suggestions."

Possible responses include the following:

a. Tell me about one person who has taken over a small part of your suggestion.

or

b. Well, you could say to that person what you just said to me, and see how they respond. Tell me what you think they might say.

4. Stating Goals for Future Growth

Once the interviewee has clarified his or her present state as a helper, the last few minutes of the interview will focus on where he or she wants to go from here. The interviewer will elicit material that fills in the blanks for the two goal statements shown below.

Goal 1   I want to _____

so that _____.

Goal 2   I want to _____

so that _____.

NOTE: Remember, the first half of the goal statement must include an action verb.

DESCRIPTION OF EXERCISE

Form small groups of four or five persons.

In your groups, ask one person to be the helper while a second person (the presenter) tells his or her story about his or her development as a helper, including beliefs, turning points, and unique outcomes.

The other group participants act as observers, being alert to the strengths or resources that are apparent by watching the presenter work, and focusing on the clarity of the goal statements that are generated.

The focus of the observers is actually two-fold: (a) to take note of the resources that the presenter mentions, and (b) to notice the nonverbal cues that showed increases in the presenter's energy.

One observer will act as the timekeeper by stating: "You've worked for 15 minutes"; and, "It's time to wrap it up now."

(Even a gesture involving placing one hand across the other to form a T can be used to signal that 20 minutes has passed.)

FLOW CHART

Planning session (2-3 minutes)

1. Select a presenter who will talk about his or her development as a helper.
2. Select an interviewer.
3. Select observers.

Working session (20 minutes)

The interviewer elicits the presenter's history as a helper, focusing on strengths, unique outcomes, and positive beliefs.

Debriefing session (15 minutes)

The debriefing session offers the observers an opportunity to practice sending reflective messages to the presenter. Such messages emphasize what the observer experienced as the interview progressed. They always start with the pronoun "I" and are followed by words such as:

"I was impressed by. . . ."
"I was struck by. . . ."
"I noticed that. . . ."

The content of your messages may include:

A. Positive resources you saw in the interview.
B. Speculations about how a resource might be used to reduce an obstacle.
C. Significant nonverbal cues noticed in the interview.
D. A new way of stating the goal.

APPLICATIONS IN THE REAL WORLD

As a helper you will often reflect to your clients regarding how you are experiencing them in an interview. These reflections will be a vital part of your total influence with a client.

EXERCISE 2:
LEARNING TO USE ENACTMENT IN A HELPING SESSION

PURPOSE

To identify the skills needed to move a helping session from a verbal interaction to some form of dramatic enactment. The enactment experience can include a demonstration of how two or more people tend to interact with each other and how they might interact in a more functional way.

DESCRIPTION

In a group of five or six trainees, ask for two volunteers, one to play a mother and one to play a father.

The two volunteers and the observers will be asked to read the script below. The two volunteers will then continue the interaction from the end of the script, with a third volunteer acting as a helper.

SCRIPT

Mother: Well, I need help. I'm struggling to find some way to deal with my 13-year-old. He won't obey any of my rules at home, like curfew or doing chores I give him, or even doing his school work before he watches TV. I call my husband at his work, but even though he says I'm right, he doesn't help in any way. He works about 12 to 14 hours a day and doesn't get home until after Joe (the son) has gone to bed.

Father: I don't know what she expects from a 13-year-old boy. He's rebelling, naturally, like all boys do.

Mother: Well, you won't even help me with any rule I have. Joe is going to flunk out of school, the way he's going. He even stays out past his curfew.

(Start the role play)

PROCEDURE

Let the enactment run for 5 to 7 minutes. The observers are then asked to reflect on what they saw occur in the enactment, using reflective messages as described in Exercise 1. After the reflections, each participant is asked to write down what he or she would say to the couple in the next minute. A volunteer is then requested to use his or her own intervention with the couple to see where the enactment might go. After one or two minutes, the enactment is stopped and another volunteer tries an intervention. This segment of the exercise will close after approximately four interventions have been tried.

DEBRIEFING

After three or four interventions have been used in brief enactments, the entire group debriefs the total exercise. Particular emphasis is placed on asking the "husband and wife" what they experienced in relation to each episode: what was different; what was their internal experience like; and what they would have liked to have been used as an intervention.

The entire exercise would be closed by identifying the significant things learned by participants and how enactments could be used in future real-life helping sessions.

EXERCISE 3:
PRACTICING TRANSFORMING

PURPOSE

To learn to evolve problem material so that the outcome is a well-formed goal statement.

DESCRIPTION

In pairs, each person will act as either a helper or a helpseeker for approximately 20 minutes. (Roles will be reversed for the second half of the exercise.) The helpseeker will talk about a problematic relationship he or she would like to change.

Examples

A person who is constantly belittling your work.

Two of your children who are constantly fighting.

An adolescent who never appreciates your efforts as a parent.

A parent who continues to treat you like a child, even though you're over 30.

PROCEDURE

One participant (the helpseeker) will present the problem situation, with the second person acting as the helper. Whenever a problem word or a problem-focused sentence is stated, the helper uses one of the responses below.

1. Seeking the Opposite State

Example questions:

A. When your sons are fighting, what do you want them to be doing instead?

B. If this problem did not exist, what would your relationship be like?

C. When was there one time that this problem did not occur?

2. Providing the Opposite State

Example statements:

A. I gather that you want your sons to get along more often and to fight less often.
B. And you want this person to be showing appreciation for your work rather than belittling it.
C. So you feel abused emotionally in this relationship, and you want to feel that this person is appreciating you.

PROCEDURES

This process of using these two types of responses works best in a stop-start format. That is, stop the interview each time you have used either questions that seek the opposite state or statements that provide the opposite state, and you have received a response from a helpseeker. The two of you can then discuss how well your intervention worked and what else the helper could have said. Then, continue the interview until you use another transforming intervention, and follow the same process.

After 10 to 12 minutes, switch roles and follow the same process as described above.

CLOSING THE EXERCISE

Notice that in each of the examples in 2 above, the key problem word has been transformed into an opposite way of acting. This transforming skill can be practiced by you on your own by taking common problem words and asking yourself, "What would be the opposite actions?" The three problem words in the examples are shown below, with the three opposite behaviors on the right.

fighting	cooperating
belittling	appreciating
abused	respecting

PRACTICE FOR YOU

Please try to describe the opposite actions for the words below, and then compare your words with those provided.

stealing
lonely
depressed
frantic
quarrelsome
violent
scornful
rejecting

Answers for the items above

stealing	giving
lonely	interacting
depressed	expressing
frantic	calm
quarrelsome	agreeing
violent	self-restraining
scornful	accepting
rejecting	tolerating

You may have used other words that are just as appropriate as those provided. What is most important in the words you wrote is that they can be visualized as actions, so that you will know when someone is doing what the word implies. Look at your list and see if you can change any word that describes a condition into an action. Compare your words with your partner, so that you end the exercise with a clear understanding of the use of transforming as a skill.

EXERCISE 4:
OBSERVING DIFFERENCES

PURPOSE

Learning visual concentration.

DESCRIPTION

Participants pair up and sit facing one another. Each person carefully observes the person opposite her and notes dress, hair, jewelry, and so on. Participants then turn their backs on each other and change three things on their person.

Participants then face each other again. Each person must identify what changes his or her partner has made.

Participants are then asked to change partners and told to change four things.

Continue the exercise by changing partners three or four more times, and increasing the number of changes to seven or eight.

NOTE FOR FACILITATOR

This exercise emphasizes creativity and concentration, so you don't want to help with suggestions of changes, such as shoes untied, watch changed to other hand, and so on. The participants' energy will tend to go up as you increase the number of changes, which is very desirable as part of the exercise. Don't let participants know in advance that you will be increasing the changes. As the changes increase, participants will see things they did not notice at first glance, thus increasing their observation skills. This has been called the Survival Game.

EXERCISE 5:
LEARNING TO READ GESTURES

PURPOSE

To enhance honest communication between two people. This skill is particularly important when conducting a silent interview, as well as in verbal helping sessions.

DESCRIPTION

With a partner, establish some kind of imagined relationship, such as teacher-student, husband-wife, and so on. Then decide on some important message to be communicated between the two of you, and a reply. The message should be of vital concern to both of you in your relationship. When you are both clear about the message and the reply, work out a dance-like scene in which you communicate the message and the reply, using only physical gestures. Treat the scene seriously and do not limit yourself to "normal" or realistic gestures. Your gestures (including facial expressions) will provide significant emotional communication.

Note: The word *emotion* means, literally, outward movement.

Example:

There is a knock at the door. Two adult siblings look at each other and gesture to communicate their emotions about who is on the other side.

VARIATIONS

Practice three or four different gestures for the same situation until you find gestures that most fully communicate what you wish to have happen between the two of you.

EXERCISE 6:
EXPERIENCING GOAL-DRIVEN BEHAVIOR

PURPOSE

To learn how the desire to accomplish a goal provides the energy to direct a two-person interaction.

DESCRIPTION

With a partner, choose a common everyday role, such as a student, a customer, a housewife, and give that person a goal such as an improved grade, a loan from a bank when you have no collateral, or a pothole in your street you want fixed. The goal must require interaction with another person. For the partner with the goal, have him or her write the first part of a goal by completing an "I want" or "I wish" sentence. Don't worry about the second part of the goal statement; that is the part that comes after the "so that." [See part 4 of exercise 1 to clarify writing goal statements.] Then identify who they will have to interact with to accomplish the goal.

Act out the situation in which the person seeks to achieve his or her goal. Carry out the interaction for 2 or 3 minutes, and stop the action during the interaction.

DEBRIEFING

Analyze what happened during the interaction. In particular, look for what influenced the behavior of the person seeking a goal. Was it the actions of the other person or external stimuli, or internal decisions? Also, look at the written goal statement, which will probably be only partially complete. Identify the larger goal, that is, the second part of the goal statement that comes after the words "so that." See how the immediate actions of the goal seeker fit or do not fit with this larger outcome.

After this analysis, reverse roles and identify a new role, and go through the same steps as described above.

CLOSING THE EXERCISE

In many books on helping interviews, the authors talk about "finding out what is really going on" regarding a problem situation. These authors focus on eliciting a person's internal feelings as a way to find out what is going on.

This exercise is intended to help participants look at how a person's goal or intent drives an interaction between two people.

To close the exercise, identify, within each pair of participants, examples from real life in which goal-driven behavior best explains the way each partner acted in a two-person interaction. If the exercise has been done in a large group, have some of these examples shared in the total group.

REFERENCES

Berg, I. K. (1994). *Family-Based Services.* New York: Norton.

Covey, S. R. (1990). *The Seven Habits of Highly Effective People.* New York: Fireside.

de Bono, E. (1990). *I Am Right, You Are Wrong.* New York, NY: Viking Penguin.

de Shazer, S. (1988). *Clues: Investigating Solutions in Brief Therapy.* New York: Norton.

Dilts, R. (1990). *Changing Belief Systems with NLP.* Capitola, CA: Meta Publications.

Hoffman, L. (1993). *Exchanging Voices: A Collaborative Approach to Family Therapy.* London: Karnac Books.

Hoyt, M. (Ed.) (1994). *Constructive Therapies, Volume I.* New York: Guilford.

Miller, S. D., Hubble, M., & Duncan, B. (Eds.) (1990). *Handbook of Solution Focused Brief Therapy.* San Francisco: Jossey-Bass.

O'Hanlon, W. H., & Weine-Davis, M. (1989). *In Search of Solutions: A New Direction in Psychotherapy.* New York: Norton.

Reimers, S., & Treacher, A. (1995). *Introducing User Friendly Family Therapy.* New York: Routledge.

Satir, Virginia. 1983. *Of rocks and flowers.* Videotape. Golden Triad Films.

Steinbeck, J. (1939/1993). *The Grapes of Wrath..* New York: Knopf.

White, M., & Epston, D. 1990. *Narrative means to therapeutic ends.* New York: Norton.

INDEX

ABOUT THE AUTHOR

Frank F. Maple is Professor of Social Work at the University of Michigan School of Social Work. In his current position, he specializes in the use of technology for the teaching/learning process in methods classes on interviewing, group work, and family therapy. He has published six software programs titled *Goal-Focused Therapy* and has produced five interactive videodiscs under the same title. His other publications include *Shared Decision Making* and *Dynamic Interviewing: An Introduction to Counseling,* and he is the coeditor (with Rosemary Sarri) of *The School in the Community.*